Mystagogia

THE JOURNEY CONTINUES

Easter to Pentecost

Alonso de Blas, O.F.M.

Cycles:
B - 2008
C - 2009
A - 2010

Tau-publishing.com

Mystagogia, The Journey Continues
Published by Tau publishing
Phoenix, Arizona 85006

ISBN 978-0-9815190-5-0

Edited by: Jeffrey Campbell
Book Layout and Design: Arlene Besore
Cover Art: Ronda Millea

Printed in the United States of America

2008—First Edition

10 9 8 7 6 5 4 3 2 1

For re-orders and additional inspirational books, CD's, Cards and Calendars visit our website at Tau-publishing.com.

INTRODUCTION

As we begin this joyous new season of the Church year, the Easter season, we should call to mind the regard in which our early church held it. It was so important to them, that they were able to offset their centuries-old respect for the Sabbath, good Jews that they were, and began instead to observe every Sunday as the Lord's Day, calling it a "little Easter." The only-just-now-concluded Sacred Triduum is the centerpoint of the entire church year. All other seasons lead to it or flow from it. As we saw it, the Christian Easter fulfilled and replaced the Jewish Passover, which took place on the 14th day of the month of Nisan, to be commemorated with a yearly observance on that date. But the powerful, life-changing experience of that Easter Sunday made for a conflict in our primitive church: what to honor, the fixed date of the saving death of the Lamb of God, as was their ancestral Passover custom? Or the Sunday that marks the Father's raising of Jesus to new life? A Sunday, of course, would complicate matters, because it would not reappear conveniently on the exact date year after year. But the tremendous impact of that Easter Sunday's events would carry the day, and our calendar would be set up so as to lead to an Easter feast observed on the Sunday after the first full moon after the spring equinox. Complicated, yes—but beautiful, no?

So we begin the church year by introducing the arrival of the promised Messiah, the four Sundays of Advent leading to Christmas on the 25th of December, the fixed date for the celebration of Jesus' birth as one of us, as Emmanuel (God-with-us). Once the Advent/Christmas season concludes with the feast of the Baptism of the Lord, which initiates his public career of announcing and initiating the kingdom of God, the so-called "Ordinary Time" of the church year begins on the next day, Monday of the First Week in Ordinary Time. After that first week ends, the next Sunday will be reckoned as the Second Sunday in Ordinary Time, and so on till forty days before Easter Sunday, when "Ash Wednesday" issues in the season of Lent, leading up to the Sacred Triduum.

Still with me? After these three sacred days, the shortest but most intense season of the church year, we find ourselves where we are today (like the "You Are Here" arrows on a map), beginning a fifty-day prolongation and savoring of our Easter joy. The Greek name for it, in our early church, was the mystagogia, a period given over to the deepening of the impact of Easter on the lives of our newly-received members from Holy Saturday Night's initiation. It was like having these newborns marinating in the Holy Spirit, soaking up adult-ed-level instruction and experience, then further instruction with further experience, till they celebrated at Pentecost the wonderful, wonder-filled experience of the Holy Spirit's power at work in them and in the church. Pentecost was the pinnacle of Jesus' production. Remember how the church used to speak of the three eras in our salvation history? [1] The era of the Father-Creator covered the seven days, if you're a stickler for the printed word, of creation. Or the seven stages of untold millennia, if you consider the meaning (and not just the surface) of the words used to recount the process of God the Father's creation of all things. [2] Then the era of the Son-Redeemer covered the traditional thirty-three years of Jesus' life among us, working to bring about our salvation. And [3] the third era, of the Holy Spirit-Sanctifier, extends from Pentecost, when he is sent to be our Paraclete/Protector, till the end of time, when the process of our growth in holiness will culminate in our invitation to our home in heaven with God! It's interesting that Jesus first ascends to heaven, so he and the Father—acting in unison—can send us their Spirit, that binds them together in mutual love, so we can become active, and grow, in our love-binding unity as the body of Christ.

Anyway…back to our calendar-making. Scenario A: If the number of ordinary weeks (begun after Christmas season, interrupted by Lent and the Triduum, and continuing after Pentecost now till we reach the mandated four Sundays in Advent to prepare for Christmas) totals thirty-four, then after Pentecost the interrupted series of Ordinary Sundays takes up the count where it left off before Ash Wednesday. For example, if the Sunday before Ash Wednesday had been the Seventh Sunday in Ordinary Time, then the Mass of Monday after Pentecost would be from the weekdays after the Eighth Sunday in Ordinary Time. The following Sunday would continue the count and be the Ninth Sunday in Ordinary Time, but it gives way to the feast of the Most Holy Trinity, followed by the Tenth, which is replaced by the feast of the Most Holy Body and Blood of Christ. By the next Sunday we've run out of special feasts associated with Easter/Pentecost, so it reverts to its plain-vanilla title: the Eleventh Sunday in Ordinary Time. And so it goes, until the 34th and final Sunday in Ordinary Time, which is always celebrated as the feast of Christ the King. And by the next Sunday, we're back in Advent, starting all over again.

Scenario B: If the number of ordinary weeks is thirty-three, we skip the first week that would normally follow Pentecost, as we had explained above. So the Monday after Pentecost would come from the weekdays after the Ninth (skip the Eighth) Sunday in Ordinary Time. That way the 34th and final Sunday in Ordinary Time will leave room for the four Sundays of Advent before December 25th, and all's well that ends well. [P.S. Remember the choice of day (Sunday) over date (Passover 14th Nisan)? The spring equinox falls on a fixed date, March 21/22, but waiting for the full moon and then the Sunday following, leaves a range of possible calendar days, pre-determining Ash Wednesday (its necessary starting-point), earlier in 2008 (Feb. 6) and later in 2009 (Feb. 25).]   You got all that? Move to the head of the class! If not, re-read slowly, or just wait for the church bulletin to tell you what's next. At least this way, you know why.

So here we are, finally, at the

Monday in the Octave of Easter

Scripture

Acts of the Apostles 2:14, 22-32 *[On Pentecost] Peter addressed [the crowd], "You who are Jews, indeed all of you, listen! Jesus was a man whom God sent to you with miracles, wonders and signs as his credentials. These God worked through him in your midst, as you well know. He was delivered up by the set purpose and plan of God, [who] freed him from death and raised him up again, for it was impossible that death should keep its hold on him. David says of him: "I have set the Lord ever before me, with him at my right hand I shall not be disturbed. My body will live on in hope, for you will not abandon my soul to the nether world, nor will you suffer your faithful one to undergo corruption." David was a prophet and knew that God had sworn to him that one of his descendants would sit upon his throne. He said that he was "not abandoned to the nether world," nor did his body "undergo corruption," thus proclaiming beforehand the resurrection of the Messiah.*

Responsorial Psalm 16: 1-2, 5, 7-8, 9-10, 11 (the source of Peter's quote above)

Matthew 28: 8-15 *The women hurry away from the [empty] tomb half-overjoyed, half-fearful, and ran to carry the good news to his disciples. Suddenly, Jesus stood before them and said, "Peace! [Tell] my brothers that they are to go to Galilee, where they will see me." The guards told the chief priests what had happened, and were given a large bribe to tell everyone, "his disciples came during the night and stole him while we were asleep."*

4

Reflection

Peter is so taken by the Spirit that he unbolts the windows, opens the balcony and steps out boldly to address the crowd. He reminds them of the wonders and works performed by Jesus in their midst. He assures them that what befell Jesus was part of God's plan, so much so that Jesus counted on his Father's protection even as bad things happened to him. And so the prophecy of David's Psalm 16 comes to fulfillment, because God is so impressed by Jesus' loving trust that he must rescue him from that death that Jesus had accepted in loyalty to his Father's call. This same loving rescue will be ours if we have the same loving loyalty to God's plan, and let nothing come between us and his will. That's a lot harder than it sounds, right? But we know that Jesus rose, and how he came to rise. Don't be afraid—the Holy Spirit will inspire and enable us to answer with Jesus.

In Matthew's telling of the Resurrection, the women react with fear and joy to the empty tomb, and when Jesus manifests himself to them they lose the fear, and in joy embrace his feet. They receive the charge of going to his brothers to direct them to where they would see him. Is that clear enough for us? When we are lucky enough to see the Lord and embrace him, our natural response is to make the same wonderful experience possible for our brothers, the rest of Jesus' family. When will the others see the Lord and embrace him? When we bring Jesus to them, with arms open in acceptance, forgiveness, and love, and bring his peace-giving embrace to them. We are as much as there is physically of Jesus in this world, now that he's gone home to his Father.

Tuesday in the Octave
of Easter

Scripture

Acts of the Apostles 2: 36-41 *Peter said to the Jews: "Know beyond any doubt that God has made both Lord and Messiah this Jesus whom you crucified." They were deeply shaken [and] asked, "What are we to do?" Peter answered, "You must reform and be baptized, that your sins may be forgiven; then you will receive the gift of the Holy Spirit."*

Responsorial Psalm 33: 4-5, 18-19, 20, 22

John 20: 11-18 *Mary [Magdalen] stood weeping beside the tomb. Jesus [was] standing there, but she did not know him. He asked, "Why are you weeping?" She supposed he was the gardener [and] said: "Sir, if you are the one who carried him off, tell me where you have laid him and I will take him away." Jesus said to her, "Mary!" She turned to him and said [in Hebrew] "Rabboni!" (meaning "Teacher"). Jesus then said: "Go to my brothers and tell them I am ascending to my Father and your Father, to my God and your God!"*

Reflection

It turns out, Peter tells them, that the Jesus they crucified was Lord and Messiah! How can they possibly make up for that awful wrong decision? Remember the Creed: "We believe in one baptism, for the forgiveness of sins." Strange, not the Sacrament of Reconciliation, but Baptism brings us the forgiveness of our sins. Of course, if you've put Jesus to death, you can't undo that. But...you can choose to enter into his death with him, by undergoing Baptism, so that you die as well...so as to rise as well. His Spirit will bring him to life in you, to risen life in you.

In John's Gospel today we have a tender scene. Poor Mary is so distraught she doesn't even recognize Jesus next to her. When she hears him call her name she responds immediately, and hugs him out of sheer joy. He asks her to let go of him and let him go…to his Abba who is now our Abba as well. She must let go of him as she had known him, in his human form, because now he has been called home by his Father, who has become, by Jesus' saving death for us, our Father as well. Talk about a silver lining….

Wednesday in the Octave of Easter

Scripture

Acts of the Apostles 3: 1-10 *When Peter and John were going up to the temple for prayer [they met] a man crippled from birth being carried in. He begged them for alms, hoping to get something. Peter said, "I have neither silver nor gold, but what I have I give you! In the name of Jesus Christ the Nazarean, walk!" He began to walk around [and] went into the temple with them—walking, jumping about, and praising God. [And] the people were struck with astonishment.*

Responsorial Psalm 105: 1-2, 3-4, 6-7, 8-9

Luke 24: 13-35 On late afternoon of Easter Sunday, two disciples are returning home to Emmaus, sadly trying to digest all the events of the days just past. Jesus joins them, but does not allow them to recognize him as they speak. He chides them for not realizing that the Messiah had to undergo all these things so as to enter into his glory, and *"beginning with Moses and all the prophets, interpreted for them every passage of Scripture which referred to him."* As they approach their village, he coyly makes as if to continue on the road, but they invite him to stay over with them after they shared their evening meal. *"When [Jesus] had seated himself with them to eat, he took bread, pronounced the blessing, then broke the bread and began to distribute it to them. With that their eyes were opened and they recognized him; whereupon he vanished from their sight."* They said, *"Were not our hearts burning inside us as he talked to us on the road and explained the Scriptures to us?"* So they immediately returned to Jerusalem to tell the Eleven and the others their meeting with the living, risen Christ.

Reflection

From our earliest days, our church is a "happening" place! Peter and John invoke the name of Jesus—meaning his person, his power, his living presence—and wonderful things happen: the same wonderful things that Jesus accomplished in his life with us are now accomplished by his followers, who represent him in his physical absence from us. Luke tells a neat story: the man, once un-crippled, not only joins in their prayer, he's joyously jumping around and praising God, in pretty un-hushed tones, you can bet. No wonder everybody notices the hubbub and recognizes he used to be the cripple who would sit begging at the "Beautiful Gate." How powerfully present Jesus continues to be in the life of his baby church. Physically, he's ascended into heaven. But sacramentally he lives in and through us—his church, his body, his extension into human history.

But he does not intrude; he always waits on our invitation. What a different story the Emmaus experience would have been had Jesus revealed himself on the road, imposing his presence upon us, as it were. How beautiful is his choice to let us invite him in, and only then allowing us to recognize his presence. What merit is there to hosting Jesus if we see him as Jesus? The fun is to recognize him after we've hosted the least of our brothers (Matthew 25, anyone?) and only then discover his presence in our brothers and sisters. And I love how the encounter ends: once they recognize him in the breaking of the bread (and isn't this just like Mass?—we hear the Word and meet him in the flesh), it's "Mission Accomplished!" and Jesus has no need to remain visible any longer. We know he's here with us, he has brought God close to us, he remains with us even if no longer visibly. What a gift is our faith!

Thursday in the Octave of Easter

Scripture

Acts of the Apostles 3: 11-26 When the crowd rushes over to check out the one-time cripple that's now dancing around, praising God, Peter rises to the occasion and preaches. "Don't look at us as if we had done this through any power of our own. It's the power of Jesus that has healed this man, the one you chose to kill even as you set free a murderer. But not to worry, you were acting in ignorance, which can now be remedied, if you recognize Jesus as the promised Messiah of God. You don't have to take our word for it, *all the prophets have announced the events of these days. You are the children of those prophets, you are the heirs of the covenant God made with your fathers.'*"

Responsorial Psalm 8: 2, 5, 6-7, 8-9

Luke 24: 35-48 Like the first reading, this one also continues yesterday's selection. The disciples arrive from Emmaus to find that some in Jerusalem have also seen Christ. And then, there he is in their midst, wishing them Peace! To convince their astonished eyes, he shows them his hands and feet, and invites them to touch him. Even better, he asks for something to eat. Now they're sure he's not a ghost, and he reminds them: *"Everything written about me in the law of Moses* *and the prophets and psalms had to be fulfilled. The Messiah must suffer and rise from the dead on the third day. In his name, penance for the remission of sins is to be preached to all the nations, beginning at Jerusalem. You are witnesses to all this."*

Reflection

The early church's preaching presented Jesus' passion and death as foreseen by the prophets. We are the ones who might associate Jesus' death with defeat. But in his mind, it's clearly a victory, the victory intended for his people by our heavenly Father. Suffering is not a curse; it's an invitation to join Jesus in carrying out the plan of forgiveness and a new start, a life that rises out of the ashes of our sinful past and takes us up into God's own holiness. It turns out that we have nothing to fear when we leave everything behind to follow Jesus. The path may be pain-filled, but it leads to glory.

Each day's gospel during this week proclaims another post-Resurrection appearance by the Lord, as if trying to extend the wonderful events of the first day throughout the entire week. Typically, the Lord appears without warning, moves quickly to convince us, wishing us peace and proving it's really him—not just a vision—by either showing them his wounded body or by eating in their presence. When the visit is over, he disappears into thin air. But it's interesting to note the Eucharistic meal-association often present. A nice reminder to us of where to find him really present—at Mass, our sharing in his banquet of love, in each other as we gather as his family.

Friday in the Octave of Easter

Scripture

Acts of the Apostles 4: 1-12 The Sadducees, unlike the Pharisees, denied the possibility of a future life, so they came to silence Peter's witness to the risen Christ. They bring him before the authorities to question him: *"By what power or in whose name have men of your stripe done this?"* Peter, filled with the Holy Spirit, answers, *"Leaders of the people! If we must answer for a good deed done to a cripple and explain how he was restored to health then you and all the people of Israel must realize that it was done in the name of Jesus Christ the Nazarean, whom you crucified and whom God raised from the dead. This Jesus is 'the stone rejected by you the builders which has become the cornerstone.' There is no other name in the whole world given to men by which we are to be saved."*

Responsorial Psalm 118: 1-2, 4, 22-24, 25-27 (the source of Peter's quote)

John 21: 1-14 This appearance takes place at the Sea of Tiberias (a.k.a. Galilee) the disciples are having some down time, and Peter, probably bored, says he's going fishing. Soon the rest follow suit, but they catch nothing all through the night. Jesus appears, unrecognized, on the shore right at daybreak and suggests they try off the starboard side. Suddenly, unexpectedly, the nets groan under the heavy load, and John is the first to catch on. "It's Jesus!" When they got to shore they found he had a small fire with a fish and some bread. He asked them to bring some of what they had hauled ashore so they could all have breakfast. *"Not one of the disciples presumed to inquire 'Who are you?' for they knew it was the Lord. Jesus came over, took the bread and gave it to them, and did the same with the* *fish."* And so went the third time he appeared to them after being raised from the dead.

Reflection

Once again, Peter finds himself in a position to proclaim the saving death of Jesus. This time the Sadducees want to mock his claim of Jesus coming back to life. But Peter is seized by the Holy Spirit, and quotes the Psalmist nicely to them, to convince them that Jesus was wrongfully judged a criminal and put to a shameful death. The Father has brought him back to life, in accord with the prophecies, and will use him as the cornerstone for the new church, the new assembly of the people being offered salvation.

In the gospel, it is once more Peter who propels the action. The others follow their leader. After a fruitless night, a voice from the not-too-distant shore suggests they try casting their net over the starboard side. The results are such an immediate contrast with what they had tried to accomplish on their own—all night long—that John makes a quick connection, and recognizes the landlubber as Jesus. (It probably didn't hurt that he was the youngest of them, and his eyesight was probably sharper than theirs.) (But it's the spiritual eyesight, the insight, that counts here.)

Notice the Eucharistic overtones of the meal-sharing. Jesus is their host, and offers them their nourishment—the fish and bread that appear in the miraculous feeding of the five thousand. The risen Savior nourishes our risen life.

Saturday in the Octave of Easter

Scripture

Acts of the Apostles 4: 13-21 The priests and elders were amazed at the self-assurance of Peter and John, realizing they were uneducated men with no social standing. Since the people were so taken with the miracle of the cripple, the authorities could do nothing to the apostles but to chastise them for spreading their story and forbid them to *"mention that man's name to anyone again."* Peter and John counter: would it be right for us to obey you rather than God? *"Surely we cannot help speaking of what we have heard and seen."* The court could find no way to punish them because of all the people who were praising God for what had happened.

Responsorial Psalm 118: 1, 14-15, 16-18, 19-21

Mark 16: 9-15 In the Vatican II Weekday Missal we read: "Mark's gospel, in most manuscripts, ends with [today's] summary of the post-Resurrection appearances of Jesus. This summary is an excellent conclusion to our Gospels of this [first] week of Easter." *"Jesus first appeared to Mary Magdalene"* but the disciples she told refused to believe her. *"Later, he was revealed to [two of] them completely changed in appearance"* but the others put no more faith in them than in Mary Magdalene. *"Finally, at table, Jesus was revealed to the Eleven. He took them to task for their disbelief and stubbornness."* Then he told them, *"Go into the whole world and proclaim the good news to all creation."*

Reflection

We have followed for days now the saga of the crippled man's return to health in the Name of Jesus, the discussion it raised among the spectators, and the consternation among the authorities, who were rattled by the tremendous impact of these lowly, uneducated men in their religious arena. And Peter, far from being cowed by these important people, stands up to them and turns every challenge into an opportunity to get out the word on Jesus to one and all, fearlessly and fruitfully. What a change in these heretofore fearful men! From denying Jesus out of fear for their own lives, they now gladly put their lives on the line to proclaim Jesus as the long-awaited, even though unacknowledged, Messiah. What a difference the Spirit makes in us, from the inside out! What power we find in Jesus' Name!

You can tell this is Mark's version of the Good News, because the disciples don't come off looking very good. They repeatedly refuse to put credence in the testimony of those whom God sends to them, and they get a dressing down from Jesus when he finally catches them all together in one appearance. But all's well that ends well: he ends up sending them out to the whole world to proclaim the good news they have witnessed. Are we up to it? Does our world hear from us about the need to repent and reform? Do we offer the world possibilities for meeting this gracious, forgiving, encouraging Lord when we go about our lives as his ambassadors—not just telling the good news, but being the good news for them that he has been for us? Seems too far out of our reach? In the power of Jesus' Name, ask the Holy Spirit to inspire His efforts in us! There is no other name by which we can be saved. Thank you, Jesus! Amen. Hallelujah!

Second Sunday of Easter

Cycle A - Scripture

Acts of the Apostles 2: 42-47 *They devoted themselves to the teaching of the apostles and to the communal life, to the breaking of the bread and to the prayers. They shared all things in common; they would sell their property and possessions and divide them among all according to each one's need. Every day they would [meet] in the temple area and [then break] bread in their homes. With exultant and sincere hearts they took their meals in common, praising God and winning the approval of all the people.*

Responsorial Psalm 118: 2-4, 13-15, 22-24

First Letter of Peter 1: 3-9 *Blessed be the God and Father of our Lord Jesus Christ, who in his great mercy gave us a new birth to a living hope through the resurrection of Jesus Christ from the dead, to an inheritance that is imperishable, undefiled, and unfading, kept in heaven for you. Although now for a little while you may have to suffer through various trials, so that the genuineness of your faith may prove to be for the praise, glory, and honor of Jesus Christ when he appears. Although you have not seen him you love him; even without seeing him you believe in him, and you rejoice with inexpressible joy because you are achieving your faith's goal, your salvation.*

John 20: 19-31 On Easter Sunday night the disciples were gathered together and locked in safely, out of fear of the Jews. Suddenly Jesus appears in their midst and greets them with the familiar *"Shalom! Peace be with you."* To identify himself, he shows them his hands and his side, and they rejoice on recognizing him. Then again, *"Peace. As the Father has sent me, so I send you."* Then he breathes on them, saying: *"Receive the Holy Spirit."* One of the Twelve, Thomas, was not there with them, and would not believe them when they told him what had happened. The following Sunday they are once more gathered—this time, Thomas included. Jesus appears and challenges Thomas, who meekly proclaims, *"My Lord and my God!"* This gives Jesus the chance to preach his encouraging beatitude: *"Blessed are those who have not seen and have believed."*

Reflection

All three readings stress the value life in the Christian community. In Acts the connection of common holdings of goods and common meals is interesting: sharing a meal in thanksgiving has as a natural consequence the sharing of other material goods. As a supernatural consequence, when you share in the Eucharist, you are sharing in the life of Jesus. And the Mass is intended for the uniting of the community in Communion; no longer do we find several priests "saying" a private Mass at a side altar, each with an altar boy to represent the people. The medieval practice of "getting in your Mass" (and, with it, your stipend) has given way to a return to our early practices, with bishops and deacons (there were no priests yet) gathering in the entire community at a family table, with Christ as the host. Today, priests will concelebrate with the community, rather than do a Mass by and for themselves, because the Eucharist is not a private celebration.

Peter's encouraging sermon is addressed to a community undergoing trials and suffering. But since it is guarded by God's power, it is achieving its goal in mutual strength.

The notorious "doubting Thomas" episode can be interpreted less as a lack of faith, and more as a sign of what we lose when we are not in community: the shared sense of the presence of Jesus. The scene allows Jesus (and John the Evangelist, who sets up the whole event) to proclaim: *"Have you come to believe because you have seen me? Blessed are those who have not seen and have believed."* And this is just the message John wants his listeners to hear. Remember his was the last gospel to appear, some thirty or forty years after the first one. By now most of the people who had been with Jesus in that room were dead…so his listeners had to stop whining about how they would have loved to have been there, and learn to spot the presence of the same Jesus in the common breaking of the bread every Sunday.

The scene of Jesus breathing on them and saying: *"Receive the Holy Spirit. Whose sins you forgive are forgiven them; and whose sins you retain are retained"* also packs a wallop. It turns out that this Greek verb <u>emphusao</u> is the same verb used in the Septuagint LXX, (the Greek translation produced by the Jews for their expanding readership) in Genesis 2:7 (God breathed into Adam's clay). And this is the only time this verb appears in the entire New Testament. Get it? In raising Jesus from the dead, we have a new Genesis: God makes a new start for all mankind; Jesus is the new Adam; we receive new life…entrusted to us! If we withhold this life from others, they remain dead; if we share it, we all come to new life together. Christian community rocks!

Second Sunday of Easter

Cycle B - Scripture

Acts of the Apostles 4: 32-35 *"The community of believers was of one heart and mind; they had everything in common. Those who owned property or houses would sell them, bring the proceeds of the sale, and put them at the feet of the apostles, and they were distributed to each according to need."*

Responsorial Psalm 118: 2-4, 13-15, 22-24

First Letter of John 5: 1-6 *Everyone who believes that Jesus is the Christ has been begotten by God. Everyone begotten of God* *conquers the world, and the power that has conquered the world is this faith of ours. Jesus Christ it is who came through water and blood—not in water only, but in water and in blood. It is the Spirit who testifies to this, and the Spirit is truth."*

John 20: 19-31 (This has been covered in p. 15, Second Sunday, Cycle "A".)

Reflection

Christ is so alive in the early church, that their beautiful unity in heart and common life remains our elusive but ever-enticing ideal, even as it flies in the face of our modern world's individualistic, acquisitive culture. This is family life at its most noble: "from each according to his ability, to each according to his need." It really is unfortunate that we've come to remember this mainly as the slogan of Soviet Communism—which was long ago revealed as the farthest thing from a family. Their "common-ism" is a claim, and a deceitful one at that. Whereas in the early church, "common-ism" was never a tool for allowing a few to live off the misery of the many. In fact, it was what a family <u>should</u> be: those with extra put it in the pot, so that those in need could take from the pot.

In John's letter we see Christ, coming as conqueror of sin and evil through water and blood, baptism and death. His submission to seeming defeat on the cross is vindicated by the waters of Baptism, which drown out our human, sinful existence and create in us a fountain of living water, the loving Spirit, whose presence we strengthen in the blood of the Eucharist, which nourishes this new life and confirms in us the Spirit's power.

Second Sunday of Easter

Cycle C - Scripture

Acts of the Apostles 5: 12-16 *"Through the hands of the apostles, many signs and wonders occurred among the people. More and more believers, men and women in great numbers, were continually added to the Lord. The people carried the sick into the street and laid them on cots and mattresses, so that when Peter passed by at least his shadow might fall on one or another of them. Crowds from the towns around Jerusalem would gather, too, bringing their sick and those troubled by unclean spirits, all of whom were cured."*

Responsorial Psalm 118: 2-4, 13-15, 22-24

Revelation 1: 9-11, 12-13, 17-19 *"I, John, your brother, found myself in Patmos because I proclaimed God's word and bore witness to Jesus. I was caught up in ecstasy and heard behind me a piercing voice which said: 'Write on a scroll what you now see.' I turned around to see whose voice it was [and] I saw seven lampstands [and] among them One like a Son of Man. I fell down at his feet. He touched me and said: 'There is nothing to fear. I am the First and the Last, and the One who lives. Once I was dead but now I live—forever and ever."*

John 20: 19-31 (This has been covered in p. 15, Second Sunday, Cycle "A".)

Reflection

Even as the reading from Revelation places us in the end-times, today's selection from Acts directs our attention to the very first days of the church, showing her to be in full and fruitful continuity of power with the Jesus of the gospel. Remember when the disciples were oohing and aahing over some miracle of Jesus and he told them that they would be doing even greater signs than those? Here you have it: Peter's <u>shadow</u>, for goodness' sake, is powerful enough to bring healing on those he walks by. With Jesus, you used to have to call on him, or at least touch him. But now the church finds Peter so filled with the Spirit's power, that it is enough for this disembodied, almost non-existent part of him to just barely come into contact, and the healing goes on! Great Scott!—or better: Great God!

John's vision echoes that of Daniel chapter 7: One like a Son of Man comes before the throne/sanctuary of God and is revealed as sharing in His power and position. John sees Jesus in the heavenly sanctuary, amid the lampstands (7) which represent the (how many?—want to guess?) 7 churches to which John addresses this message. So we see once again the overriding concern of John to have his audience come to see Jesus not as dead some sixty years before, but as alive and present in their midst, in their church, in their celebration of the sacraments.

Monday in the Second Week of Easter

Scripture

Acts of the Apostles 4: 23-31 *Peter and John, after being released, went back to their own people and told them what the priests and leaders had said. "They have brought about the very things which in your providence you planned long ago. But now, O Lord, look at the threats they are leveling against us. Grant [us] complete assurance by stretching forth your hand in cures and signs and wonders to be worked in the name of Jesus, your holy servant." The place where they were gathered shook as they prayed. They were filled with the Holy Spirit and continued to speak God's word with confidence.*

Responsorial Psalm 2: 1-3, 4-6, 7-9

John 3: 1-8 *A Pharisee named Nicodemus, a member of the Jewish Sanhedrin, came to Jesus at night. "Rabbi," he said, "we know you are a teacher come from God, for no man can perform signs and wonders such as you perform unless God is with him." Jesus gave him this answer: "I solemnly assure you, no one can see the rule of God unless he is begotten from above." "How can a man be born again once he is old?" retorted Nicodemus. "Can he return to his mother's womb and be born all over again?" Jesus replied: "I solemnly assure you, no one can enter into God's kingdom without being begotten of water and Spirit."*

Reflection

As we continue readings from <u>Acts</u> we get the sense that the Holy Spirit is the protagonist throughout. When the disciples are released from punishment, with a warning to stop, they immediately report to their mates, and draw strength from their union to renew their efforts at any opportunity. The Spirit that they stir into action by this communal prayer is so powerful that the whole building they're in starts to shake!

Typically, in John's Gospel, Jesus' opening salvo is blunt, rough-edged, easy to misunderstand. When the listener voices his confusion, this allows Jesus to explain what he means, now that he's got our attention. Nicodemus recoils at the image of being literally born all over again. But Jesus will point out what he really means: making a new beginning—water and Spirit/wind as in Genesis' original beginning. God means to afford us a whole new start, and Jesus' saving death will bring us this new life.

Tuesday of the Second Week of Easter

Scripture

Acts of the Apostles 4:32-37   (Please consult p.17—Second Sunday Cycle B.)

Responsorial Psalm 93: 1, 1-2, 5

John 3: 7-15 Jesus said to Nicodemus: "You must all be born from above. The wind blows where it will. You hear it, but you do not know where it comes from or where it goes. So it is with everyone begotten of the Spirit." When Nicodemus still protests, Jesus gets a little personal: "You hold the office of teacher of Israel and still you do not understand these matters?" Then he adds bluntly: "No one has gone up to heaven except the One who came down from there—the Son of Man. Just as Moses lifted up the serpent in the desert, so must the Son of Man be lifted up, that all who believe may have eternal life in him."

Reflection

The Greek word pneuma can mean wind, or air, or breath. The Latin is spiritus, spirit, the breath of life, the power of the wind. You don't comprehend (understand, contain) the Spirit—it contains (comprehends, encircles) you! God gives his life as he wills, and sends his Son to prepare us for the Spirit's coming upon/into us. Jesus, sent from God, is being rejected by his own people. So we're reminded of the paradox of the saraph snakes in the desert: when the Israelites complained, they received them as punishment, and when they repented, they were to look on a bronze replica of the same critter that had hurt them, so that now it could save them. Jesus will be seen as a complete failure, but those who recognize him as the one sent from above for our salvation, and lay claim to it, will be saved when he is raised on the cross, like that serpent on a pole. What had meant pain and suffering now becomes salvation and new life.

Wednesday of the Second Week of Easter

Scripture

Acts of the Apostles 5: 17-26 The high priest and his fellow Sadducees were jealous of the disciples' success in preaching. So they had them arrested and jailed. But during the night an angel of the Lord came and led them out, saying: *"Go and take your place in the temple precincts and preach to the people all about this new life."* They did just that. When the entire Sanhedrin met to deal with them, they found out that even though the place was locked and guarded, the disciples weren't inside! In fact, they could see them back at their old post by the temple. So they sent the captain with the guard to arrest them again. They brought them in, but without any show of force, for fear of being stoned by the crowd, that's how popular they had become.

Responsorial Psalm 34: 2-3, 4-5, 6-7, 8-9

John 3: 16-21 *God so loved the world that he gave his only Son, that whoever believes in him may not die but may have eternal life. God did not send the Son into the world to condemn the world, but that the world might be saved through him. The light came into the world, but men loved darkness rather than light, because their deeds were wicked. Everyone who practices evil hates the light; he does not come near it, for fear his deeds will be exposed. But he who acts in truth comes into the light, to make clear that his deeds are done in God.*

Reflection

The Jewish religious authorities are so jealous of the disciples' ever-growing popularity that they have them arrested first, and then plan to meet the next day for trial. God takes the initiative, however, and has an angel deliver them from imprisonment, with orders to take up their posts their next chance. They happily do so. The next morning guards are sent to bring them in from prison but they're gone! Even though the place was guarded all night! Then they are seen still at it, and are brought in again, but gently, so as not to upset the crowds surrounding them. The Holy Spirit fills them with courage, and delivers them from shackles, because he has work for them to do: get the word out! Do we have it in us to do likewise? We have the same Holy Spirit in us, sending us on the same errand.

John continues his report on the conversation between Jesus and Nicodemus. As we will increasingly notice, in John's gospel a dialog with Jesus soon becomes a monolog by Jesus. The questioner fades out of the foreground as Jesus clarifies his point and explains what his words really mean. He came to bring, not condemnation, but salvation to the world. The judgment we'll receive results from our own choice: we step into the light of Jesus and act honorably, or we slink off into darkness so we can "get away with" doing nasties. What a wonderful opportunity to walk in the light—with Jesus, back to the Father. Or, unfortunately, to prefer the darkness so we can continue our life of sin and shame—away from Jesus and the Father who sent him to rescue us. What a shame to forget that, thanks to Jesus' saving death, we are not our own any longer: we belong to him, he redeemed us, and at a great price. Our physical bodies weigh us down and make it seem as if we belong to this world. But Christians know we belong to God. We may walk on earth, but we live a heavenly life.

Thursday of the Second Week of Easter

Scripture

Acts of the Apostles 5: 27-33 *Before the Sanhedrin, the high priest [interrogated them], "We gave you strict orders not to teach about that name, yet you have filled Jerusalem with your teaching, and are determined to make us responsible for that man's blood." To this, Peter replied: "Better for us to obey God than men! The God of our fathers has raised up Jesus whom you put to death. He whom God has exalted is to bring repentance to Israel and forgiveness of sins. We testify to this. So too does the Holy Spirit, whom God has given to those that obey him." When the Sanhedrin heard this, they were stung to fury and wanted to kill them.*

Responsorial Psalm 34: 2, 9, 17-18, 19-20

John 3: 31-36 *The One who comes from above is above all [and] testifies to what he has seen and heard. He does not ration his gift of the Spirit. The Father loves the Son and has given everything over to him. Whoever believes in the Son has life eternal.*

Reflection

Peter and John do not back down when threatened by the authorities. They have a higher loyalty that keeps them from obeying these men. They announce instead that forgiveness is possible, and that if they had obeyed God they too would have received his Spirit. The Sanhedrin does not expect this, and are stung to the quick. Only the crowd's high regard for the disciples allows them to get out with their lives.

How can Jesus speak this way about God? Because he knows him, he comes from him, sent by him to give testimony—better, to give us the same gift of Spirit that joins him to the Father, so that we too can become children of God, and no longer just creatures of the Creator. This gift is not measured out carefully to us, not rationed. It is poured into our hearts, so that with Jesus, whom the Father has rescued from death by filling him with the Spirit, we too can be filled (after we die to ourselves and to this world) with the same life-giving Spirit.

Friday of the Second Week of Easter

Scripture

Acts of the Apostles 5: 34-42 The wise Gamaliel, member of the Sanhedrin and renowned teacher (Saul, soon to become Paul, was one of his students) called for calm by reminding them that if the disciples are operating from human strength, they'll fall by themselves, but if the source of their activity and power is from God, the Sanhedrin would be foolish to attempt to quell it with violence. "Just give it time—leave them alone and see what comes of this." They grant his point, but still can't resist giving the apostles a good old-fashioned whuppin' before dismissing them, with orders to never repeat Jesus' name. For their part, the apostles left, full of joy that they had been found worthy of a beating for the sake of the Name. And after leaving they began again to preach far and wide the good news of Jesus the Messiah.

Responsorial Psalm 27: 1, 4, 13-14

John 6: 1-15 A vast crowd follows Jesus, wowed by the signs he kept performing for all their sick. Jesus sees how many needy people are gathered around and asks (rhetorically, it turns out) what the disciples could do about feeding them. After much head-scratching they report there's a young boy there with five barley loaves and two dried fish—but what good would that do? Jesus goes "hmm," and tells them to get the people to recline, to get ready to eat, all five thousand of them! *Jesus then took the loaves of bread, gave thanks, and passed them around to those reclining there; he did the same with the dried fish, as much as they wanted.* When they'd all had enough, he asked his disciples: "gather up the crusts that are left over so that nothing will go to waste," and twelve baskets are filled by the leftovers of five loaves among five thousand! When the people saw that and figured out what had happened, they wanted to carry him off with them (for the next time they got hungry?), so Jesus fled back to the mountain by himself.

Reflection

Nothing can stop the apostles. Peter is brought before the equivalent of our Supreme Court, but he won't give in. Cooler heads prevail when the mood gets dangerous for our boys. But even then, they are punished for their uppityness before being released with a warning. Do you think that'll stop us? No way! The power of the Holy Spirit is upon us, and, as for the spanking—it has the opposite effect: the apostles are overjoyed that they get to suffer as they give fearless witness to Jesus, just as he had suffered in giving witness to his Father's love for the world.

We know the miracle of the multiplication of loaves and fishes made a huge impact on the early church, because it is the only miracle to be mentioned in all four of the gospels. It foreshadows beautifully his use of the bread at the Last Supper to find a way to remain with us, within us, even after he is torn away from us by the authorities and hung on that cross. Should we be surprised by his claims that he is the true bread from heaven, that unlike our fathers who ate the manna in the desert to keep going, but died nonetheless, we who eat his flesh and drink his blood will never die? He is the proven master of bread, he can make it do whatever he wants. And it fits his role in our lives: how often his post-Resurrection appearances are connected to eating bread, to sharing in a meal! This is how he remains close to us, so we can approach him daily ("our daily bread") at the Table of the Lord.

Saturday of the Second Week of Easter

Scripture

Acts of the Apostles 6: 1-7 *As the number of disciples grew, the ones who spoke Greek complained that their widows were being neglected in the daily distribution of food, as compared with the widows of those who spoke Hebrew.* So the apostles assembled them and said: *"It is not right for us to neglect the word of God in order to wait on tables,"* so why don't you pick seven men who are prudent and deeply spiritual, so we can appoint them to serve you in our stead? That way we can keep concentrating on prayer and the ministry of the word. The community gladly followed this suggestion, and selected Stephen, a man filled with faith and the Holy Spirit; Philip, Prochorus, Nicanor, Timon, Parmenas and Nicolaus of Antioch, who had converted to Judaism. They then presented the seven to the apostles, who prayed over them, imposing their hands on them as a sign of delegated authority. *The number of disciples in Jerusalem enormously increased [and] there were many priests among those who embraced the faith.*

Responsorial Psalm 33: 1-2, 4-5, 18-19

John 6: 16-21 One evening, the disciples were crossing the lake toward Capernaum. It was dark, and late, and the sea was being churned by a strong wind. *When they had rowed three or four miles,* *they sighted Jesus approaching the boat, walking on the water. They were frightened, but he told them, "It is I; do not be afraid." They wanted to take him into the boat, but suddenly it came aground on the shore they had been approaching.*

Reflection

Does the "English as official language" movement in our Southwest ring a bell? Here we are with Jews divided into two linguistic groups: the Aramaic-speaking Palestinians, and the Greek-speaking returnees from the Diaspora. The solution is immediate, amicable and really a stroke of genius. The apostles stay out of it, ask those complaining to propose an answer to their problem, and lay hands on the seven selected. You know they're Greeks—check out their names. Problem solved, thanks to the Holy Spirit's guidance. Interesting that many priests are being welcomed to our group, because we will not need priests (offering bloody sacrifices at the temple) for our people. What we have is shepherds (the apostles) and their flocks (the communities they found and lead). When the need for special services arises, deacons (from the Greek, fittingly, diakonia, service) are appointed to help the shepherds with the business end of things, freeing our leaders for leadership. (Only centuries later, when we grow and spread exponentially, are priests appointed so as to help the bishops, not with the business end, but with the liturgical leadership of the communities which have grown too large to be overseen by just the one bishop in charge now of several flocks, sort of like sheepdogs working with the shepherd.)

In this gospel selection, John is showing how Jesus, just finished demonstrating his mastery over bread, again shows his power over nature, by walking on the water. Cute how, as soon as they spot him and are ready to invite him into the boat for the rest of the trip, they find that they're already at the shore they'd been rowing toward for so long. With Jesus, you get results! On your own, you've got to do a lot of hard rowing....

Third Sunday of Easter

Cycle A - Scripture

Acts of the Apostles 2: 14, 22-33 Peter stood up with the Eleven and explained to the Jews that Jesus, sent by God and thus working mighty wonders in their midst, was delivered up *" by the set plan and foreknowledge of God,"* to the death they dealt out to him. *"But God raised him up, releasing him from the throes of death, of this we are all witnesses. Exalted at the right hand of God, he received the promise of the Holy Spirit from the Father and poured him forth, as you see and hear."*

Responsorial Psalm 16: 1-2, 5, 7-8, 9-10, 11

First Letter of Peter 1: 17-21 *Realize that you were delivered from the futile way of life your fathers handed on to you, not by any sum of silver or gold, but by Christ's blood beyond all price: the blood of a spotless lamb chosen before the world's foundation and revealed for your sake in these last days. It is through him that you are believers in God, the God who raised him from the dead and gave him glory. Your faith and hope, then, are centered in God.*

Luke 24: 13-35 (It has already appeared on p. 7, Wednesday Octave of Easter.)

Reflection

The death of Jesus, especially by crucifixion, had left the disciples demoralized. But now that they've received, at Pentecost, the Advocate who reminds them of everything Jesus told them, they can assure their listeners that it all happened to fulfill God's plan, that their very scriptures foretold a suffering, redeeming Messiah. They walk in confidence on the same path Jesus trod, because they have experienced the Jesus brought back to life by the Spirit, as well as their own lives raised and renewed by the gift of the same Spirit. Not to worry—God's been in charge all along.

Peter writes to assure his readers that they are precious to God. They were ransomed from human lives of sin and death, not by mere gold or silver (still precious metals today) but by the precious blood of Christ, our saving Paschal Lamb. After his saving sacrifice, Jesus was raised by a grateful Father and given a name that is above every other: Jesus is Lord! So when we remain in union with Jesus as we are called to suffer, we await with confidence the same glorious result—the Father bringing us up to heavenly life with him.

Third Sunday of Easter

Cycle B - Scripture

Acts of the Apostles 3: 13-15, 17-19 *Peter said to the people: "The God of Abraham, of Isaac and of Jacob, the God of our fathers, has glorified his Servant Jesus, whom you handed over and disowned when Pilate was ready to release him. You disowned the Holy and Just One and preferred instead to be granted the release of a murderer. You put to death the Author of life. But God raised him from the dead, and we are his witnesses. Yet I know, my brothers, that you acted out of ignorance, just as your leaders did. God has brought to fulfillment by this means what he announced long ago through all the prophets: that his Messiah would suffer. Therefore, reform your lives! Turn to God, that your sins may be wiped away!"*

Responsorial Psalm 4: 2, 4, 7-8, 9

First Letter of John 2: 1-5 *We have, in the presence of the Father, Jesus Christ, an intercessor who is just; an offering for our sins, and* *for those of the whole world. Those who say, "I know him," but do not keep his commandments are liars.*

Luke 24: 35-48 (This was discussed on p. 9, Thursday Octave of Easter.)

Reflection

Peter is blunt in his recap of their mishandling of Jesus. But he under-stands they acted in ignorance, and extends an offer of forgiveness, encouraging them to reform now so as to receive the Holy Spirit.

John connects knowing God with keeping his commandments. Knowledge connotes the experience of God's presence, rather than just the mental concept of God. How can we claim the experience of God's presence yet fail to reflect that in our conduct? Keeping the commandments, especially to love one another as Christ has loved us, means that the love God has for us is reaching others and allowing them also to become children of the same Father. This common experience of God in the Scriptures, in community, in the Eucharist celebrated together—giving thanks to God—is what makes church happen!

Third Sunday of Easter

Cycle C - Scriptures

Acts of the Apostles 5: 27-32, 40-41 (Please review 1st readings from Thursday and Friday of Second Week of Easter, pp. 25 & 26.)

Responsorial Psalm 30: 2, 4, 5-6, 11-12, 13

Revelation 5: 11-14 John has a vision of heaven. He hears the voices of the angels and elders who surround the throne of God. Countless, they cry out in a loud voice: *"Worthy is the Lamb that was slain, to receive power and riches, wisdom and strength, honor and glory and blessing. To the One who sits on the throne and to the Lamb be blessing and honor, glory and might, forever and ever."* Adding an *"Amen!"* they all fall down in worship.

John 21: 1-14/19 (We've seen vv. 1-14 already on p. 11, Friday Octave of Easter. Verses 15-19 now follow.) *When they had finished breakfast, Jesus said to Simon Peter, "Simon, son of John, do you love me more than these?" [He] answered "Yes, Lord, you know that I love you."* A second and third time Jesus asked him the same question, so Peter was distressed, and said, *"Lord, you know everything, you know that I love you."* Jesus then proceeded to warn him about how in his death he would glorify God, and then said to him, *"Follow me."*

Reflection

In <u>Revelation</u> John describes his vision of the heavenly liturgy—dollops of praise are solemnly heaped upon the One on the throne and the Lamb next to him. All creatures sing praises, exhausting the <u>Thesaurus</u> entries on this item, and there are still not enough words we can use in singing the praises of our wonderful God. In the end, words fail, and they all simply fall on their faces and worship. What a majestic scene! I always try for a little taste of it when I pray the <u>Trisagion</u>, the old <u>Sanctus</u> of the Mass, with the "Holy" being sung in stereo: first from one side of heaven, then from the other and then again full blast by both speakers at once, as the angels attempt to give expression to the surpassing holiness of God.

I suspect that the reason for Peter's distress is that it starts to dawn on him what Jesus is doing—better yet, undoing. Remember how Peter had denied the Lord three times? OK, so here's your make-up quiz:

three times you get to acknowledge me. Now we can start over.
And if that weren't clear enough already, the last words from Jesus
are the exact first words Peter heard from him years before: "Follow
me." What a merciful God, gently but effectively restoring our
broken relationships as if nothing had ever happened.

Monday of the Third Week of Easter

Scripture

Acts of the Apostles 6: 8-15 *Stephen, filled with grace and power,
worked great wonders among the people. Members of the "Synagogue of Roman Freedmen" would engage him in debate, but they
proved no match for the wisdom and spirit with which he spoke. They
brought in people to make many false charges against him, inciting
the elders and scribes. The members of the Sanhedrin stared at him
intently. Throughout, Stephen's face seemed like that of an angel.*

Responsorial Psalm 119: 23-24, 26-27, 29-30

John 6: 22-29 After being miraculously fed, the crowd remained
on the other side of the lake. They realized the next day that the
disciples had shipped out without Jesus, but they couldn't find him,
so they sailed across the lake to Capernaum to look for Jesus. When
they found him they asked, *"Rabbi, when did you come here?" He
answered: "I assure you, you are not looking for me because you
have seen signs, but because you have eaten your fill of the loaves.
You should not be working for perishable food, but for food that
remains unto life eternal, food which the Son of Man will give you."*

Reflection

Stephen, the first of the deacons selected, proves worthy of his calling. Accused of denigrating Moses and the temple, he is able to ward off their arguments in public debate. After stirring up the people against him, they stare intently at him, but he remains unperturbed, his face like that of an angel. The Spirit is with him, so it doesn't matter who is against him.

The well-fed crowd stirs into action trying to track down Jesus the next morning. They know he didn't ship out with his disciples, but he's not there anymore, so they go to Capernaum to find him. Surprised to find him there, they ask how? But he sidesteps it and goes right to the point: "You weren't able to read the signs, you just want to eat again. Your concern should not be on food for your bodies (which I took care of yesterday) but for your life beyond. Food that won't perish, food I am prepared to give you if you can learn to see beyond, to understand when I say I am the bread of life, the bread from heaven." Jesus takes care of our physical needs not out of concern for just our bodies, but in order to show us his deeper concern for our souls, our whole person. The body is the screen on which he's showing us a movie. The screen is there, of course, but the movie carries the message.

Tuesday of the Third Week of Easter

Scripture

Acts of the Apostles 7: 51 – 8: 1 *Stephen said to the people and elders and scribes: "You stiff-necked people, uncircumcised in heart and ears, you are always opposing the Holy Spirit, just as your fathers did." "In their day, your fathers killed those who foretold the coming of the Messiah, and now it's your turn—you killed him when he came." They were stung by his words. But it got worse: he looked up to the sky and exclaimed: "I see an opening in the sky—the Son of Man is standing at God's right hand!" That did it. They rushed him, dragged him out of town and began to stone him. A young man named Saul held their coats, so they could heave the stones more easily. Dying, Stephen prays: "Lord Jesus, receive my spirit. And do not hold this sin against them."*

Responsorial Psalm 31: 3-4, 6, 7, 8, 17, 21

John 6: 30-34 *The crowd said to Jesus: "What sign are you going to perform for us to see so that we can put faith in you? Our ancestors had manna to eat in the desert; according to Scripture, 'He gave them bread from the heavens to eat.'" Jesus said to them: "It was not Moses who gave you bread from the heavens; it is my Father who gives you the real heavenly bread. God's bread comes down from heaven and gives life to the world." "Sir, give us this bread always!" Jesus explained to them: "I myself am the bread of life. No one who comes to me shall ever be hungry."*

Reflection

The Holy Spirit continues to show his power in the early church. When Stephen is hounded to death, he remains calm and strong and brave. And loving, too, because he dies asking pardon for his killers. What a hero! Our first martyr, he gives his life for Jesus, even as Jesus had given his life for the Father. Death is not defeat. It looks like defeat, but only to the world. To the believer it is the final act of faith and obedience to the same God who once began our lives and now calls us back to himself. How can we be sure? The indwelling Spirit tells us so.

The people demand a sign, so that once convinced by it, they can put their trust in him. Whoa there, big fella! That's not going to work. By definition: if you have to see it to believe it, then you're not really believing—there's no room for belief, because you've had your proof already. That's not faith, that's acquiescence, and there's a big difference there. That's like standing before the altar and telling your fiancé(e): "I tell you what—let's live together for fifty years, and then we'll come back and I'll marry you, once I've got the proof that we're good with each other." That's interest, but it's not love. That's an offer, not a commitment. God commits himself to us ever so generously. He invents us, he follows our ups and downs, always ready to get us back on track, to forgive, to give us the Food we need to be strong for our journey. Can't I commit myself to him, without putting him through any more paces, without demanding explanations?

Wednesday of the Third Week of Easter

Scripture

Acts of the Apostles 8: 1-8 *A great persecution of the church in Jerusalem [began]. Devout men buried Stephen; after that Saul began to harass the church. He entered home after house, dragged men and women out, and threw them into jail. Philip went to*

Samaria and proclaimed the Messiah. The crowds that heard him and saw the miracles he performed attended closely to what he had to say. Many who had unclean spirits, and paralytics and cripples were cured. The rejoicing in that town rose to fever pitch.

Responsorial Psalm 66:1-3, 4-5, 6-7

John 6: 35-40 *Jesus explained to the crowd: "I myself am the bread of life. I have come down from heaven to do the will of him who sent me, [namely] that I should lose nothing of what he has given me; rather, that I should raise it up on the last day. Indeed, this is the will of my Father, that everyone who looks upon the Son and believes in him shall have eternal life. Him I will raise up on the last day."*

Reflection

Even as the church comes under attack in Jerusalem, it spreads vigorously to other places. Philip creates a fuss in Samaria with all the signs and healings he performs wholesale. You can see how the Spirit's backing of these men allows them to make beachheads everywhere they go. But isn't it great how much good these missionaries are doing? It should remind of us our task, of being sent by the same Spirit on the same errand. And even if we don't feel equipped to bring about major-league healings, we can still bring pardon and peace and the proximity of God to those we encounter—and that's a lot of healing right there.

In the gospel Jesus announces himself as the middle step: the Father is the source of our life, Jesus is the strength to maintain that life, and the Spirit is our guide on the return to the source of our life, like salmon making their way back upstream. (Hey! Wasn't a fish the symbol for a Christian? But that's another story....) Jesus assures us on our Father's behalf: we believe in him (and follow his way) and he'll come for us on the last day. Now that's a lovely visual: on Judgment Day, the Judge will be coming around, making sure we're all OK, seated comfortably with a drink and snacks, as we await his official verdict. Sounds like a lock to me. How blessed we are to know Jesus as our brother, who out of love for us climbed up that hill dragging his cross, to give his life for us.

Thursday of the Second Week of Easter

Scripture

Acts of the Apostles 8: 26-40 Philip is directed by the Holy Spirit to an Ethiopian treasury official, who happened to be reading one of Isaiah's Songs of the Suffering Servant. He asks him if he understands what he's reading. No, but I'd love some help. Philip is invited to help with "Like a sheep he was led to the slaughter, like a lamb before its shearer he was silent and opened not his mouth. In his humiliation he was deprived of justice." He asks Philip whether Isaiah is saying this about himself or someone else. *So Philip launched out with this scripture passage as his starting point, telling him the good news of Jesus. As they came to some water, the [Ethiopian] said, "Look, there is some water right there. What is to keep me from being baptized?"* No sooner said than done. Immediately out of the water, Philip was snatched away by the Spirit to announce the good news at Azotus and other places until he reached Caesarea. And the new convert went happily home, rejoicing.

Responsorial Psalm 66: 8-9, 16-17, 20

John 6: 44-51 *Jesus said to the crowds: "I am the bread of life. Your ancestors ate manna in the desert, but they died. This is the bread that comes down from heaven, for a man to eat and never die. I myself am the living bread come down from heaven. If anyone* *eats this bread he shall live forever; the bread I will give is my flesh, for the life of the world."*

Reflection

Is the Holy Spirit running things or what? Unsuspecting Philip is directed to an equally unsuspecting traveler who welcomes the interest and matches it with an invitation to come on board (he was in a chariot at the time!) (Philip must have been in pretty good shape) (oh, I forgot, it was all brought about by the Holy Spirit; sorry, should've known).   Anyway, the passage is a match, natch: the Suffering Servant and Jesus. So Philip has a great time applying passages and generally filling in this foreigner on the Messiah and how he fulfills all the promises found in the Scriptures. Things were going so great that the Ethiopian spots a pool of water, stops the chariot, and receives the baptism he has been moved to request. Immediately, mission accomplished, Philip is snatched away by the Holy Spirit for a job elsewhere, and the man continues his journey overjoyed: Boy, what an entry I'm going to make in my journal when I get home tonight!

Jesus, in this typical Johannine presentation, makes startling opening moves: the bread I bring to you from my Father is my flesh. Can you see the looks on all their faces? Whaaat? Did I hear right? The dude wants us to eat his flesh and to drink his blood? If these are not the worst taboos, the most primal no-no's of society, they come pretty close, right? So what could he possibly mean? This is John's Jesus at work. His listeners are challenged, they are engaged, possibly enraged, but they're listening to find out more. And it's all good news, isn't it? I love the part about: the Father and I will come and make our abode in you. What a beautiful image! What a marvelous plus for us!

Friday of the Third Week of Easter

Scripture

Acts of the Apostles 9: 1-20 Saul is all business, totally dedicated to uprooting these new heretics, the followers of Jesus. He requested and received delegation to arrest and bring back for sentencing in Jerusalem, any followers of the way he might find in Damascus. Approaching the city, however, he is suddenly overcome by a blinding flash of light, and a voice asks: *"Saul, Saul, why do you persecute me? I am Jesus, the one you are persecuting. Get up and go into the city, where you will be told what to do."* Saul got up off the ground but was blind, so his men had to lead him by the hand. In Damascus he spent his first three days blind, neither eating nor drinking. Then the Lord appeared to the disciple Ananias in a vision, asking him to go look in on Saul. But he protested, reminding God what a dangerous man Saul was, and how much damage he had done to Jesus' followers. The Lord insisted, *"You must go! This man is the instrument I have chosen to bring my name to the Gentiles and the people of Israel. I myself shall indicate to him how much he will have to suffer for my name."* So Ananias went to Saul, laid hands on him and said, *"Saul, my brother, I have been sent by the Lord Jesus who appeared to you on the way here, to help you recover your sight and be filled with the Holy Spirit."* And immediately something like scales fell from his eyes, and he regained his sight. He got up and was baptized. Saul stayed some time with the disciples in Damascus, and soon began to proclaim in the synagogues that Jesus, the Messiah, was the Son of God.

Responsorial Psalm 117: 1, 2

John 6: 52-59 While his listeners were trying to sort out just how he could mean what he said, Jesus simply reiterates: *"The man who* feeds on my flesh and drinks my blood remains in me, and I in him. Just as the Father who has life sent me and I have life because of the Father, so the man who feeds on me will have life because of me. This is the bread that came down from heaven. Unlike your ancestors who ate and died nonetheless, the man who feeds on this bread shall live forever." And he said all this in public, in a synagogue instruction at Capernaum.

Reflection

The story of the conversion of St. Paul is a classic. Luke's pithy depiction of Saul, *"breathing murderous threats against the Lord's disciples,"* sets the stage quickly and powerfully. But God knocks him off his high horse, blinding him with light and sending him helplessly along his way. Ananias' from-the-heart objection to God's plan stands for the human reluctance to put away "justice" and learn to live in mercy, God's mercy. But he does: "Brother Saul," he addresses him. Saul has spent three days of physical and spiritual darkness, not even taking time or interest to eat or drink, thunderstruck by what has happened to him, and trying to sort it out. Then comes Ananias, healing, and baptism. All this opens a new life for him—180 degrees from his old life. Now he'll preach, not squelch, the name of Jesus. Now he'll promote, not persecute, the little church that follows Jesus. If it's true that "God writes straight with crooked lines," then this must be the greatest proof of it! This wasn't a crooked line; it was an anti-line.

I can think of two important lessons: [1] Don't be too sure that just because you mean it for God's glory, what you do will be pleasing to him. You've got to be able to step back and listen to what the Spirit might be calling you to do—differently or maybe even the opposite. And [2] do not judge! Can you see with God's eyes, what purpose God might have in another person's life or activities or changes therein? State your case, but don't be too sure that's the only correct version of what's really happening. If we invite God into our lives and receive him in the Eucharist and try to carry Him, not ourselves, out from church back out into the world...we'll be helped along the right track.

Saturday of the Third Week of Easter

Scripture

Acts 9: 31-42 The Holy Spirit is going full throttle now. The church is at peace, growing in numbers and holiness. Peter releases Aeneas, a paralytic who's been bedridden for eight years, from his sad plight: *"Aeneas, Jesus Christ cures you! Get up and make your bed."* Word of this gets around quickly and many more are converted to the way. On another occasion Peter gets word from the disciples that Tabitha, a very worthy and hard-working member of their church, needed him. He arrives at her home, is welcomed and shown some of the many garments she had made when she was still with them, then is taken to her room, where she is laid out on her bed, dead. He sends every one out, kneels and prays. Then: *"Tabitha, stand up."* She opens her eyes, looks at him, and sits up. He helps her to her feet, and calls in all her friends, to show them she was alive. The news spread throughout Joppa, and because of it, many came to believe in the Lord.

Responsorial Psalm 116: 12-13, 14-15, 1-17

John 6: 60-69 *Many of the disciples of Jesus remarked, "This sort of talk is hard to endure! How can anyone take it seriously?" Jesus was fully aware that his disciples were murmuring in protest at what he*

*had said. "Does it shake your faith?" he asked them. "It is the spirit
that gives life; the flesh is useless. The words I spoke to you are spirit
and life. Yet among you there are some who do not believe." From
this time on, many of his disciples broke away and would not remain
in his company any longer. [He] then said to the Twelve, "Do you
want to leave me too?" Simon Peter answered him, "Lord, to whom
shall we go? You have the words of eternal life. We have come to
believe; we are convinced that you are God's holy one."*

Reflection

In his gospel, Luke chronicles the life of Jesus in the flesh, his physical
presence among us. In Acts, he chronicles the life of Jesus in his
church, his living presence in the world now that he has physically
been raised to the right hand of the Father's throne. His power is
constantly—in fact, increasingly—on display in the early church. Peter
doesn't do it; he calls upon Jesus to do the healing: *"Jesus Christ
cures you!"* (Don't you love the "and make your bed"? Bet those
linens could use a breather after eight years!) (Just kidding.) (I hope.)
But Jesus does not just bring us remedies to make our life better. He
offers us a whole new life, so Peter will bring sweet, hard-working
Tabitha back from death. How much clearer could it be? The Spirit
makes Jesus present through the presence of his church at work.
Then, it was Peter and the church disciples. Now, it is Benedict XVI
and the church disciples. It's the same church. It's the same Holy
Spirit empowering us to become and act like—better: to act in the
name of—the same Jesus. How are we doing?

Today's gospel scene is dramatic. People find it too hard to make
(human, reasonable) sense of Jesus' words, so they leave him. Jesus
will not back off. He offers a challenge; in fact, he gets in their faces,
"Do you want to leave me too?" He's tried to point out to them that
the flesh is useless, that human reason will not work here. His words
are spirit (not flesh) and life. Peter latches on to that phrase in his
pledge to stay: *"You have the words of eternal life."* Not because he

understands, but because he's willing to respond in the faith that Jesus is asking of him. It would be easier if we could get God to explain himself to us (as if that were possible!—how could we ever understand/comprehend/get a handle on God?). In any case, that would be giving him the agreement of only our intellect, and not the loving, trusting hearts that he desires from us.

Fourth Sunday of Easter

Cycle A - Scripture

Acts of the Apostles 2: 14, 36-41 *[At Pentecost] Peter stood up with the Eleven, raised his voice and addressed them: "Let the whole house of Israel know beyond any doubt that God has made both Lord and Messiah this Jesus whom you crucified." When they heard this, they were deeply shaken. They asked Peter and the other apostles, "What are we to do, brothers?" Peter answered: "You must reform and be baptized in the name of Jesus Christ, that your sins may be forgiven; then you will receive the gift of the Holy Spirit."*

Responsorial Psalm 23: 1-3, 3-4, 5, 6

First Letter of Peter 2: 20-25 *"Do put up with suffering for doing what is right. Christ suffered for you in just this way, and left you an example to follow. When he was insulted he returned no insult. Instead, in his own body he brought your sins to the cross, so that all of us, dead to sin, could live in accord with God's will. By his wounds you were healed. At one time you were straying like sheep, but now you have returned to the shepherd, the guardian of your souls.*

John 10: 1-10 *Jesus spoke to them in the figure of a shepherd with his flock. He calls his sheep by name, and leads them out and they follow him, because they recognize his voice. [The disciples] did not* *grasp what he was trying to tell them. He therefore said [to them again]: "I am the gate. Whoever enters through me will be safe."* The thief comes to steal and destroy. *"I came that they might have life and have it to the full."*

Reflection

We return to Peter's Pentecost preaching. He offers his listeners a solution: reform and be baptized and receive the Spirit. First comes conversion: they must turn from their life of sin, centered on themselves, and open themselves to the new life, focused on the risen Jesus. This is the salvation promised by the Father from long ago. If you die to this life, you will live in the Spirit!

Our psalm is David's grateful praise for the God who shows himself as the most loving and caring shepherd, dealing gently and generously with us, his own flock. Peter's letter asks his readers, who are undergoing severe trials in their churches in Asia Minor, to follow the gentle and generous example of Jesus, *"the shepherd and guardian of your souls,"* who took our sins to that cross so they would die with him, so we could live—newly forgiven—gathered in to life with God.

The early church's most popular depiction of Jesus is as the Good Shepherd. In our first burial places, the catacombs in Rome, the walls are covered with the figure of Jesus with a lamb lovingly on his shoulders. That's how they pictured him taking their loved ones home to safety. Here he assures his followers that he cares for them, that no danger will come over them, because he is the sheepgate: out in the fields, shepherds would gather their little flocks at night, roll up brush and tumbleweeds into a makeshift corral, and lie down to sleep across the opening, to guard their charges through the night. Jesus, our Good Shepherd, puts his body on the line for us. What a charming (but foreboding) visual! What love!

Fourth Sunday of Easter

Cycle B - Scripture

Acts of the Apostles 4: 8-12 *Peter, filled with the Holy Spirit, spoke up: "Leaders of the people! Elders! If we must answer today for a good deed done to a cripple and explain how he was restored to health, then you and all the people of Israel must realize that it was done in the name of Jesus Christ the Nazarean whom you crucified and whom God raised from the dead. In the power of the name this man stands before you perfectly sound. This Jesus is 'the stone rejected by you the builders which has become the cornerstone.' There is no salvation in anyone else, for there is no other name in the whole world given to men by which we are to be saved."*

Responsorial Psalm 118: 1, 8-9, 21-23, 26, 29 (the source of Peter's quote)

First Letter of John 3: 1-2 *See what love the Father has bestowed on us in letting us be called children of God! We are God's children now; what we shall later be has not yet come to light. We know that when it [does] we shall be like him, for we shall see him as he is.*

John 10: 11-18 *Jesus said, "I am the good shepherd [who] lays down his life for the sheep."* The hireling works for pay, not from concern for his sheep, so when he sees the wolf coming he runs away, leaving them to be snatched and scattered. *"I am the good shepherd. I know my sheep and my sheep know me in the same way that the Father knows me and I know the Father; for these sheep I will give my life. There are other sheep, not in this fold, that must hear my voice and follow me, so that there shall be one flock, then, one shepherd."*

Reflection

Jesus is alive and active—in his church, just not in his physical presence any more. But he is so palpable in this typical healing of a cripple, accomplished in the power of his name, his (non-physical) presence. He's still coming close to us, in our sins, and freeing us from the bonds that hold us back from living fully. There is no salvation in anyone else. Only he can bring us to the Father with him. "No one comes to the Father except through me."

And he doesn't just bring us into proximity to the Father; he makes us children of his own almighty Father. When you pray, he tells us, start by calling him your Father, because that's how I know him, and I have made you my brothers and sisters by the gift of the Spirit of Love that binds me to the Father and the Father to me.

Jesus embodies the ideal qualities of a shepherd: constant vigilance, fearless courage and patient love for his flock. And the claims he makes here are actually Messianic. It turns out that, way back in chapter 34 of Ezekiel's prophecy, Yahweh has manifested his displeasure in the mismanagement of his people at the hands of their leaders, who instead of helping his flock, are helping themselves to it! He seethes in anger and announces that he himself will come to shepherd his people! And here comes the Messiah, the new and super David (himself a one-time shepherd [cf. today's psalm]), claiming for himself the title of the "Good Shepherd," what a true shepherd ought to be. Not only that, he also claims, *"This is why the Father loves me, because I lay down my life in order to take it up again. No one takes it from me; I lay it down freely. I have the power to lay it down, and to take it up again. This command I have received from my Father."*

Fourth Sunday of Easter

Cycle C - Scripture

Acts of the Apostles 13: 14, 43-52 Paul and Barnabas came to Antioch and worshipped at the synagogue. Many Jews and devout Jewish converts believed, and were urged to hold fast to the grace of God. The next Sabbath almost the whole city showed up. When the Jews saw the size of the crowd they became very jealous and countered with violent abuse whatever Paul said. He finally told them: *"The word of God has to be declared to you first of all; but since you reject it and thus convict yourselves as unworthy of everlasting life, we now turn to the Gentiles. For thus were we instructed by the Lord: 'I have made you a light to the nations, a means of salvation to the ends of the earth.'"* The Gentiles were delighted at this development, and accepted their message with grateful praises. And so the word of the Lord spread throughout the area.

Responsorial Psalm 100: 1-2, 3, 5

Revelation 7: 9, 14-17 [In his vision] John saw a huge crowd, totally beyond counting, made up of people from every nation and race and language, standing before God's throne and the Lamb, dressed in long white robes and holding palm branches. One of the elders said to him: *"These are the ones who have survived the great period of trial; they have washed their robes and made them white in the blood of the Lamb. He who sits on the throne will give them shelter. The Lamb on the throne will shepherd them and lead them to springs of life-giving water, and God will wipe every tear from their eyes."*

John 10: 27-30 Jesus said: *"My sheep hear my voice. I know them and they follow me. I give them eternal life, and they shall never perish. No one shall snatch them out of my hand. My Father is greater than all, and there is no snatching out of his hand. The Father and I are one."*

Reflection

Paul is forced to leave the unwelcoming Jews behind, and turns to the eager-to-welcome Gentiles. Even as he quotes Scripture to justify this move, he's not comfortable with it, and will always continue to go first to the synagogues, wherever his travels take him, and only then to the public squares to preach Jesus to all.

We must remember that John was the youngest of all the apostles, and how old he got to be before he died. (They had tried to kill him by dumping him into a vat of boiling oil, but he just emerged with a healthy tan, so instead they exiled him to Patmos.) He writes this book in the 90's, the time of the Domitian persecution. His vision assures him of the victory (palm branches) of those suffering persecution and death. Their lives are renewed, washed clean in the blood of the Lamb, who now becomes their Shepherd and leads them to water, and safety, and life. Remember how the original "blood of the lamb" figures in the Exodus story? Its blood, sprinkled on their doorposts and lintels, is the signal for the angel of death to pass over their homes and strike the firstborn sons of the other (unmarked) houses. That blood freed them from slavery in Egypt to freedom in their new land. This blood of a sacrificial Lamb ensures their passage from this world of sin into life beyond this world, with God.

How comforting, the promise that "there is no snatching out of the Father's hand," that we are brought to complete safety by following our Good Shepherd home. The only disheartening thought is that it remains entirely possible that we will choose to leave that safety by sinning. No outside influence is strong enough to undo God's protection, but we can make the mistake of leaving his protective embrace to go out and seek our own way, the way that feels good to us. Big mistake! We must not only pray "but deliver us from evil," but also speak out, by word and behavior, a timely warning for each other when we come "into temptation."

Monday of the Fourth Week of Easter

Scripture

Acts of the Apostles 11: 1-18 The church in Jerusalem heard that Gentiles, too, had been offered the saving message. So when Peter returned they complained: *"You entered the house of uncircumcised men and ate with them [shame on you!]."* Peter explained step-by-step what had led up to that. He was in Joppa, praying, when he was given a vision. Something like a big sheet was lowered to him by its four corners, and when he looked in he saw birds and animals. A voice told him to eat, and he said, "No way; nothing unclean or impure has ever entered my mouth." But the voice said, "How can you call unclean what God has purified?" This happened three times, and then the whole thing was drawn back up into the sky. Just then three men sent to me from Caesarea showed up, and the Spirit told me to follow them without hesitation. We entered the man's house, and he told us that he had seen an angel, who told him to send off to Joppa for Simon Peter, because "in the light of what he will tell you, you will be saved, and all your household."

"As I began to address them," Peter continued, the Holy Spirit came upon them, just as it had upon us at the beginning. Then I remembered what the Lord had said: 'John baptized with water but you will be baptized with the Holy Spirit.' If God was giving them the same gift he gave us when we first believed in the Lord Jesus Christ, who was I to interfere with him?" When they heard this, they stopped their objection, and began to give glory to God in these words: "If this be so, then God has granted life-giving repentance even to the Gentiles."

Responsorial Psalms 42: 2-3 & 43: 3, 4

John 10: 1-10, which has already appeared in Cycle "A," p. 45. In the "A" year, to prevent repetition, this gospel will be replaced by John 10: 11-18, which has already appeared in Cycle "B," p. 47.

Reflection

The Holy Spirit is once again leading this fledgling church. We come to a pivotal moment in our early history. A whole lot of future will depend on which path is taken at this fork in the road. The old guard, all converts from Judaism, cannot believe that Peter has ignored the ancient taboos against mixing with Gentiles, the uncircumcised, the unclean. How could you do that? Peter tries to calm them down by making a short story long. He was at prayer; he had a weird vision (his reaction must have pleased the Jerusalem group); there was a call for him, which the Spirit urged him to answer. That's why he entered the house of a Gentile, who had also been granted a vision, so God must be working through him, too. Anyway, when he sees the same Spirit poured out on them that had been poured out on the church, he figured rightly that God must be behind it all. The home boys see the logic in his procedure, and marvel that God is so cool that he extends a welcome not just to the good guys, but to the (ugh) unclean, uncircumcised outsiders, too. What wonderful news: no more walls dividing people; we are all loved by the same God, so we must no longer question anyone's worth. If God finds us all worth loving, then who are we to declare anyone unworthy of our love?

Tuesday of the Fourth Week of Easter

Scripture

Acts of the Apostles 11: 19-26 Some of the disciples, who had come from Cyprus to Antioch, began to announce the good news of Jesus to the Greeks in the city, bringing about a great increase in believers. When news of this development reached Jerusalem, they sent Barnabas to look into things. He rejoiced at how the church was growing, and urged them all to remain firm in their commitment to the Lord. Then he went to Tarsus to bring Paul back with him to Antioch, where for a whole year they met with the church and instructed great numbers. By the way, it was here in Antioch that the disciples first came to be called Christians.

Responsorial Psalm 87: 1-2, 4-5, 6-7

John 10: 22-30 (This has been considered already, on p. 49, Fourth Sunday "C.")

Reflection

Once more we return to the first major difficulty facing our baby church. What to do about Gentile outsiders coming in? Shouldn't they be circumcised first thing? That would go a long way toward removing their uncleanness. What about their dietary habits? Surely the Law of Moses came from God, too. Why should it not apply to them? The authorities in Jerusalem, of course, had no experience of the wonders of huge numbers of converts wanting to be received. They felt charged with not allowing the message of Jesus to be diluted as it spread. But the experiences of the missionaries who return with powerful witnessings assure them that God is at work in these new entries, and that God didn't seem to consider their outside-the-Law status an obstacle to his grace. If God is so visibly reaching out, who are we to not open our arms as well? Thanks be to God for the leadership of these Spirit-led and Spirit-filled missionaries.

Wednesday of the Fourth Week of Easter

Scripture

Acts of the Apostles 12: 24 – 13: 5 Barnabas and Paul return to Jerusalem, bringing John Mark along. The Holy Spirit indicated he had more work awaiting Paul and Barnabas, so they all, after fasting and praying, imposed hands on them and sent them off. They set sail for Cyprus, and when they arrived at Salamis, proclaimed the word of God in the Jewish synagogues.

Responsorial Psalm 67: 2-3, 5, 6, 8

John 12: 44-50 *Jesus proclaimed aloud: "Whoever puts faith in me believes not so much in me as in him who sent me; and whoever looks on me is seeing him who sent me. Whoever does not accept my words already has his judge, namely the word I have spoken—it is that which will condemn him on the last day. For I have not spoken on my own; no, the Father who sent me has commanded me what to say and how to speak."*

Reflection

The word of God is growing stronger in the church, which is spreading it throughout the Mediterranean. And Jesus reminds us that once we get the word out, no one will have to judge the listeners—they will have to answer for rejecting the word of Jesus, because it is the word of God that he speaks, the message of the Father's forgiving love that he announces. God will not have to judge us; our own actions will judge us: do we accept the word of Jesus that the Father's love is universal and that therefore ours should be universal also? Or do we refuse to love that way, and continue to block the message of the loving Spirit that Jesus breathed into us when he rose and came into our midst, filling us with his peace?

We read in the Vatican II Weekday Missal: "This last public teaching of Jesus ends the 'Book of Signs,' (chapters 1-12), the first part of the gospel. The miracles of Jesus were signs of the Word of God in this world. So the person who does not accept Jesus in faith is rejecting the Father who sent Jesus into the world."

Thursday of the Fourth Week of Easter

Scripture

Acts of the Apostles 13: 13-25 On his First Missionary Journey Paul comes to another Antioch, in the region of Pisidia, and enters the synagogue. After the readings, he is invited to share his thoughts with them. He launches into a recap of their history, from God's dealings with the patriarchs, the exodus, their land, Saul and David, and David's promised descendant, heralded by John who offers a baptism of repentance, and points to Jesus as the Messiah.

Responsorial Psalm 89: 2-3, 21-22, 25, 27

John 13: 16-20 *[After Jesus had washed the feet of the disciples he said:] "Blest will you be if you put [all these things] into practice.*

My purpose here is the fulfillment of Scripture: 'He who partook of bread with me has raised his heel against me.' I tell you this now, before it takes place, so that when it takes place you may believe that I AM."

Reflection

Paul is a guest at the synagogue, so he is treated courteously and invited to make himself known to all. He begins at the very beginning, obviously hoping to lead them to see the coming of Jesus as the natural conclusion to this long history of Yahweh's saving dealings with his people. We'll see how it turns out.

(Chapters 13-20 of John's gospel are called the "Book of Glory," because they present the glorious passion, death and resurrection of the Lord.) Having washed their feet, Jesus reminds the disciples that he, their master and teacher, comes not to be served but to serve. And he asks them to not just notice, but to take up his example and do likewise. He knows they will be upset at Judas' betrayal, so, to prepare them, he quotes Ps. 41. Then, when they stop to think about it, they'll still be able to believe he was not trapped by some greater power. No, he went to his death voluntarily, out of obedience to the Father and love for us.

Friday of the Fourth Week of Easter

Scripture

Acts of the Apostles 13: 26-33 Paul takes up the history of God's dealings with his people at the point of Jerusalem's failure to recognize Jesus as the Christ. Their killing him did nothing but to fulfill all that had been prophesied about the coming Messiah. But God raised him from the dead and his disciples witnessed his appearances. *"We ourselves announce to you the good news that what God promised our fathers he has fulfilled for us in raising up Jesus, according to the second psalm: 'You are my son; this day I have begotten you.'"*

Responsorial Psalm 2: 6-7, 8-9, 10-11 (the source for Paul's quote)

John 14: 1-6 *Jesus said to his disciples, "Do not let your hearts be troubled. Have faith in God, and faith in me. In my Father's house there are many dwelling places; otherwise how could I have told you that I was going to prepare a place for you? I am indeed going to prepare a place for you, and then I shall come back to take you with me, that where I am you also may be. You know the way that leads where I go." "Lord," said Thomas, "we do not know where you are going. How can we know the way?" Jesus told him: "I am the way, and the truth, and the life; no one comes to the Father except through me."*

Reflection

Even when confronted with antagonism, or worse, indifference, Paul remains loyal to his roots, and will always open his preaching of Jesus with an outreach to the Jews of the place. Here he leads them down salvation way to the appearance of Jesus, the awful mistake of not recognizing him, and therefore putting him to death, but thanks to the re-appearances of Jesus raised from death, the disciples can witness to his presence and power in the church. Ever the teacher, he quotes David's second psalm so they can hear the prophetic testimony of the great king in whose image a greater king is to come.

Today's gospel opens the beautiful "Farewell Discourse" of the Lord, preparing his friends for his departure from them (chapters 14-17). When he leaves us, he assures us, he's only going away to make preparations for our long-term stay with him. He won't leave us behind, because he will send a Paraclete (Greek for: advocate, one who looks out for you, who speaks on your behalf) that will bring to mind everything he ever told us, therefore making him present to us in that way. Of course, they won't get any relief from this promise until they experience the coming of the Holy Spirit upon them in that upper room. But then…(stay tuned for nine more days).

Saturday of the Fourth Week of Easter

Scripture

Acts of the Apostles 13: 44-52 (p. 49 Fourth Sunday of Easter, Cycle "C")

Responsorial Psalm 98: 1, 2-3, 3-4

John 14: 7-14 *"If you really knew me, you would know my Father also. Whoever has seen me has seen the Father. The words that I speak are not spoken of myself; it is the Father who lives in me accomplishing his works. Believe me that I am in the Father and the Father is in me, or else, believe because of the works I do.*

Reflection

Jesus gives expression to the profound unity between the Father and himself. He assures his disciples that, from getting to know him, they have come to know the Father. At the same time, he challenges them to believe that nothing of what he says is from himself—he is a mouthpiece for the Father's message to us. And if we find it difficult to go along with those words sometimes (e.g. chapter 6 "how can he give us his flesh to eat?"), we have only to look at his works, to realize that all he does is done for the Father, in the Father's name. No doubt, he is the legitimate article. He can talk the talk, because he walks the walk.

The "fun" part for us is to realize that he warned us: "As the Father has sent me, so now I send you." It took a lot of energy, a ton of sacrificing love, for Jesus to carry out this errand from the Father. Now he is asking us—not just the priests and bishops and religious—but all of us baptized into his body, the church, to get the same job done for one another. We are to be the words of God that the world needs to hear: words of love, patience, encouragement, forgiveness, understanding. We are to back up those words with works: doing not what we feel like doing, but what we know God has equipped us to do by granting us the guidance of the Holy Spirit and the strength of the daily Eucharist. Get going! Good luck!

Fifth Sunday of Easter

Cycle A - Scripture

Acts of the Apostles 6: 1-7 (p. 28, Saturday of the Second Week of Easter)

Responsorial Psalm 33: 1-2, 4-5, 18-19

First Letter of Peter 2: 4-9 *Come to the Lord, a living stone, rejected by men but approved and precious in God's eyes. You too are living stones, built as an edifice of spirit, into a holy priesthood, offering spiritual sacrifices acceptable to God through Jesus Christ. For Scripture has it: "See, I am laying a cornerstone in Zion, an approved stone, and precious. He who puts his faith in it shall not be shaken." The stone is of value for you who have faith. For those* without faith, it is rather, "A stone which the builders rejected that became a cornerstone." *You are "a chosen race, a royal priesthood, a consecrated nation, a people he claims for his own to proclaim the glorious works" of the One who called you from darkness into his marvelous light.*

John 14: 1-12 (Friday & Saturday of Fourth Week of Easter pp. 57 & 58)

Reflection

Peter uses a very strong and concrete image: Jesus is the once-rejected cornerstone for a whole new edifice, made up of other living stones who come close to him in answer to his call to follow. From Israel, we have inherited the same call of God's choice—we are God's Plan B, as it were. Plan A was to have Christ accepted by his people, leading them, and then reaching out to all the world, in a return to the Father. Once rejected by his own, he has made a new people his own—us, the outsiders. But the lines of the plan remain Jewish: Jesus, recognized by us as the long-awaited Messiah for the Jews, will include us in his mission, so that now, by our Baptism, we share with him the role, honor, and responsibility of being "priest, prophet, and king."

The Chrism of our Baptism marks us as baby Messiahs, wannabes, but it works on us as it worked on Jesus, marking him as the Christ, the One Anointed for a special task. By our sharing in the Spirit of Jesus we come to share in his Messianic mission of service, by virtue of being marked, christened into the Christ who is priest, prophet, and king. This famous passage from Peter is the basis for our concept of "the priesthood of all the faithful," our reminder to every member of the church of the dignity and challenge of our own Messianic call by virtue of our being baptized into the body of Christ.

Fifth Sunday of Easter

Cycle B - Scripture

Acts of the Apostles 9: 26-31 *When Saul arrived back in Jerusalem he tried to join the disciples there; but it turned out that they were all afraid of him. They even refused to believe that he was a disciple. Then Barnabas took him in charge and introduced him to the apostles. He explained to them how on his journey Saul had seen the Lord, who had conversed with him, and how Saul had been speaking out fearlessly in the name of Jesus at Damascus. Saul stayed on with them, moving freely about Jerusalem and expressing himself quite openly in the name of the Lord. He even addressed the Greek-speaking Jews and debated with them. They for their part responded by trying to kill him.*

Responsorial Psalm 22: 26-27, 28, 30, 31-32

First Letter of John 3: 18-24 *Little children, let us love in deed and in truth and not merely talk about it. His commandment is this: we are to believe in the name of his Son, Jesus Christ, and are to love one another as he commanded us. Those who keep his commandments remain in him and he in them. And this is how we know that he remains in us: from the Spirit that he gave us.*

John 15: 1-8 *Jesus said to his disciples, "I am the true vine. Live on in me, as I do in you. No more than a branch can bear fruit of itself apart from the vine, can you bear fruit apart from me. I am the vine, you are the branches. He who lives in me and I in him, will produce abundantly, for apart from me you can do nothing.*

Reflection

Luke now centers his attention on the career of the Apostle to the Gentiles, St. Paul. Since he traces him from the start, he still has the name Saul. Thanks to Barnabas the rest of the Jerusalem church learns to trust his conversion, which he demonstrates ably by his debates with local Jews, who end up clearing him entirely of suspicion, by their angry intent to kill him in order to silence him.

Don't you just love the pithy charge of the aged St. John to his listeners? Let's love in deeds, not just in words! We know what Jesus asked us to do: to love one another as he had loved us. There you have it, plain and simple. Simple…but not easy. And yet he enables us to carry out his command by placing in our hearts the powerful Spirit who brings to mind everything he said and did for us, and who prompts us to follow up not just with admiration but with taking part.

Jesus employs an engaging metaphor, familiar to his audience. He is the vine, provider of the life taken from the soil to spread to the branches. We are the branches, who take what we receive and produce the crop. Any branch damaged, or severed from the vine, will quickly wither and die. Only branches in union with the vine, branches that allow the life-juices to flow through them, will produce the grapes. What a mystery! That God uses us to reach out to others in his name and in his power, with his presence. What a wonder! That we are able to use our puny human love to contain and carry God's Love, the Holy Spirit, the giver of Life, to spread over all the world.

Fifth Sunday of Easter

Cycle C - Scripture

Acts of the Apostles 14: 21-27 Paul and Barnabas continue their missionary journey, reassuring their converts and encouraging them to persevere in the faith: *"We must undergo many trials if we are to enter into the reign of God."* After prayer and fasting, they put elders in charge of their little flocks and commend them to the Lord in whom they had placed their faith. Finally, on their return to Antioch *they called the congregation together and related all that God had helped them accomplish, and how he had opened the door of faith to the Gentiles.*

Responsorial Psalm 145: 8-9, 10-11, 12-13

Revelation 21: 1-5 *I, John, saw new heavens and a new earth. The former heavens and the former earth had passed away, and the sea was no longer. I also saw a new Jerusalem, the holy city, coming down out of heaven from God, beautiful as a bride prepared to meet her husband. I heard a loud voice from the throne cry out: "This is God's dwelling among men. He shall dwell with them and they shall be his people, and he shall be their God, who is always with them. He shall wipe every tear from their eyes, and there shall be no more death or mourning, crying out or pain, for the former world has passed away." The One who sat on the throne said to me, "Behold! I make all things new!"*

John 13: 31-33, 34-35 *Jesus said, "My children, I am not to be with you much longer. I give you a new commandment: Love one another. Such as my love has been for you, so must your love be for each other. This is how all will know you for my disciples: your love for one another."*

Reflection

In his description of life in our primitive church, Luke includes itineraries of Paul and Barnabas' missionary travels and travails—and, of course, wonderful results as well. Our little church grows, led and protected by the Holy Spirit. And not only where it was planted, but in the places to which they transplanted it, under the impetus of the Spirit. A report to the folks back home ends this typical selection.

The last book of the Bible was written in a complicated, highly symbolic style, using visions to give clandestine encouragement to the disciples being persecuted, visions which presage their eventual victory over all persecution. This highly visionary, dramatic, enigmatic style is called apocalyptic, from the Greek for: hidden, mysterious. In fact, the book used to be called "The Apocalypse of St. John," but has come to be known popularly as "The Book of Revelation of St. John," referring to the message which all these visions and highly stylized details will reveal—the victory of the Lamb!

John is graced with a glimpse of the triumphant church, no longer in anguish, beautifully dressed as a bride to meet her husband. Everything new and improved, as advertisers so often claim: new earth, new heavens, new outlook (no more pain or tears or anguish). God's promised salvation is finally here: "This is God's dwelling among us!" God will be always with us, comforting us, renewing us: "I make all things new!"

On Holy Thursday night, Judas leaves and Jesus gets down to brass tacks. It's as if he's dictating his last will and testament. "Since I don't have that much more time with you, I'll give you my last request, and I'll make it short and sweet: love one another as I have loved you." That's it. At the end of three years of going around preaching, the final chance at a message gets it across in concentrated form—just love each other, but use my love for you as your pattern. Tall order. Easily said, but hardly done. And yet, there it stands, clear as any target you'd ever want to aim at. How can we succeed at something so very noble and holy? Well, we can start by trying, and then asking for his help as we run into difficulties. It beats just standing back and figuring it's beyond our limited abilities. We need his strength? We've <u>got</u> his strength: in the Eucharist, in his presence wherever two or three are gathered, in his body the church, in his words passed on to us in the Bible.

Monday of the Fifth Week of Easter

Scripture

Acts of the Apostles 14: 5-18 While in Iconium, Paul and Barnabas learn of serious threats on them by the populace and the authorities, so they move on. At Lystra Paul notices a cripple listening intently, so he calls out to him: *"Stand up! On your feet!"* He does, to the crowd's amazement. They figured their gods had come to visit them, and they dub Barnabas Zeus, and Paul Hermes. Our boys, of course, immediately counter with: *"We are only men, human like you. We are bringing you the good news that will convert you from just such follies as these to the living God, 'the one who made heaven and earth and the sea and all that is in them.'"*

Responsorial Psalm 115: 1-2, 3-4, 15-16

John 14: 21-26 *Jesus said to his disciples: "Anyone who loves me will be true to my word, and my Father will love him; we will come to him and make our dwelling place with him. The word you hear is not mine; it comes from the Father who sent me. This much I have told you while I was still with you; the Paraclete, the Holy Spirit whom the Father will send in my name, will instruct you in everything and remind you of all that I told you."*

The church faces persecution and misunderstanding, but the message goes out, interest is piqued, and instruction follows. The Spirit guides and makes fruitful the efforts and sacrifices of our missionaries. Interesting detail on the Lycaonians' initial reaction: these must be our gods finally showing up! And the shocked and lightning-fast rebuttal from Paul and Barnabas, who proceed to name the real God responsible for the cure, with lots more explaining and enlightening over the next few hours and days, you can bet.

Jesus continues his leave-taking of the disciples. The reassuring image of Jesus and the Father taking up residence with those who love them and keep their word is followed by even more reassurance: the Paraclete, the Holy Spirit, will come upon us to remind us of Jesus' message, making him present to us, even in his physical absence from us.

Tuesday of the Fifth Week of Easter

Scripture

Acts of the Apostles 14: 19-28 (p. 63, Fifth Sunday of Easter, Cycle "C")

Responsorial Psalm 145: 10-11, 12-13, 21

John 14: 27-31 *Jesus said to his disciples: "'Peace' is my farewell to you; my peace is my gift to you. Do not be distressed or fearful. You have heard me say, 'I go away for a while and I come back to you.' If you truly loved me you would rejoice to have me go to the Father, for*

the Father is greater than I. I tell you this now, before it takes place,
so that when it takes place you may believe."

Reflection

The Hebrew <u>shalom</u>, we are told, goes far beyond peace as the
absence of war. It means the balanced relationship that is the result
of proper behavior, loving attitude, concern for well-being, etc. In
the Hebrew world, it was wished from one to another both in greeting and in farewell. Jesus wants his disciples to not be shook by his
absence from them. As he speaks these words, he's referring to his
seeming final separation as he's taken from them and killed on the
cross. But looking forward we know he really means it to calm us
from our fears when, after multiple post-resurrection appearances,
he is taken from our sight in being taken up to his Father's right hand,
to return again the <u>parousia</u>, the last day.

Wednesday of the Fifth Week of Easter

Scripture

Acts of the Apostles 15: 1-6 Some converts from Judaism were
teaching that uncircumcised converts could not be saved unless they
submitted to Mosaic laws. Paul and Barnabas and other missionaries
to the Gentile world disagreed. So they returned to Jerusalem and
convened with the apostles and elders, who were delighted to hear
of the wonderful conversion of the Gentiles. They decided to look
into the matter and pray for guidance from the Holy Spirit.

Responsorial Psalm 122: 1-2, 3-4, 4-5

John 15: 1-8 (p. 61, Fifth Sunday of Easter, Cycle "B")

Reflection

The problem of Gentiles (uncircumcised, untamed in dietary and many other practices) being received into our church was our first great crisis. Up to that point, we shared a strong, traditional, homogeneous set of religious beliefs and practices. The missionaries clearly see God's hand pointing them toward the Gentiles, once their Jewish audience shuts them off. But do we have to make them jump through Jewish hoops to reach the salvation Jesus offers? Didn't Jesus fight all his life against the formalism of the Pharisees, and the idea that we earned out salvation by our following of the Law? Hmmm. Stay tuned.

Thursday of the Fifth Week of Easter

Scripture

Acts of the Apostles 15: 7-21 Peter spoke to the assembly of apostles and elders, reminding them that God had selected him to bring the gospel message to the Gentiles. *"God, who reads the hearts of men, showed his approval by granting the Holy Spirit to them just as he did to us. He made no distinction between them and us, but purified their hearts by means of faith also. Why, then, do you put God to the test by trying to place on the shoulders of these converts a yoke which neither we nor our fathers were able to bear? Our belief is rather that we are saved by the favor of our Lord Jesus,* *and so are they."* At that, everyone fell silent, and Paul and Barnabas recounted the signs and wonders that God had worked among the Gentiles through them. James gives his support to Peter, quoting Scripture: *"I shall return and rebuild the fallen House of David. Then the rest of mankind, all the pagans who are consecrated to my name, will look for the Lord, says the Lord (Amos 9: 11-12)."* He decides to not cause them any difficulties, and instead instruct them to simply *"abstain from anything contaminated by idols, from illicit sexual union, from the meat of strangled animals, and from eating blood."*

Responsorial Psalm 96: 1-2, 2-3, 10

John 15: 9-11 *Jesus said to his disciples: "As the Father has loved me, so I have loved you. Live on in my love [by keeping] my commandments, even as I have kept my Father's commandments, and live in his love. All this I tell you that my joy may be yours and your joy may be complete."*

Reflection

Our first reading recounts what becomes known as the "Council of Jerusalem" in 49 A.D. Peter eloquently presents his case, seconded by the reports of Paul and Barnabas. James, leader of the Jerusalem community, relies on Scripture to show the way, and will make things easy for incoming Gentiles, holding them to just the basic dietary and marriage laws that Jews everywhere have always been known to live by, the traditional requirements of alien residents in Jewish lands.

This gospel is the natural extension of the vine-branches lesson in unity, showing love to be the life-source shared by God and all who love him, beginning with his Son. Jesus is so overjoyed at his unity of love (Holy Spirit) with his Father, that he wants all of us in on the same treat. We are included in the Father/Son Bond of the Spirit if we accept and work with Jesus as our brother.

Friday of the Fifth Week of Easter

Scripture

Acts of the Apostles 15: 22-31 The church in Jerusalem sent its formal decision to *"the brothers of Gentile origin in Antioch, Syria and Cilicia."* Not wanting them to be disturbed by the demands of some who *"without any instructions from us"* insisted on the observance of the Law of Moses before conversion to Christ, they send them this message: *"It is the decision of the Holy Spirit, and ours too, not to lay on you any burden beyond that which is strictly necessary, namely, to abstain from meat sacrificed to idols, from blood, from the meat of strangled animals, and from illicit sexual union. You will be well advised to avoid these things. Farewell."*

Responsorial Psalm 57: 8-9, 10-12

John 15: 12-17 *Jesus said to his disciples: "This is my commandment: love one another as I have loved you. There is no greater love than this: to lay down one's life for one's friends. You are my friends if you do what I command you. I no longer speak of you as slaves, for a slave does not know what his master is about. Instead, I call you friends, since I have made known to you all that I heard from my Father. It was not you who chose me, it was I who chose you to go forth and bear fruit. The command I give you is this: that you love one another."*

Reflection

The Spirit's calm leadership is obvious in the church's first council. The problem is presented, sides are heard, matters are taken into thought, the Spirit is called upon, and the result is: amicable, Scripture-based, satisfying, a win-win in today's lingo.

Jesus says it so simply, we almost don't have enough time to let it sink in. What a change! From slaves being told what to do, to friends who are let in on reasons why or why not. From the other side of the table, busy bringing and taking, to this side of the table, leisurely enjoying all the treats, conversation, and intimacy. Not because we longed so much for this invitation, much less deserve it in any way, but simply because God chooses to call us to closeness with him. Stop and think: out of aaaaaaaall the creatures in this world, we are the only ones who share with God the ability to know and, in response to that knowledge, to choose the good. There you have it, the reason for lifting the requirements of the Law off the backs of our incoming converts: there's nothing we can do that will earn us our salvation, no list of goodies to do or baddies to avoid—it's simply the result of God's free and gracious gift to us. What a load off our shoulders! What a loving God we have! What confidence in us when he asks us to love one another as he has loved us!

Saturday of the Fifth Week of Easter

Scripture

Acts of the Apostles 16: 1-10 At Lystra, Paul recruits a young disciple named Timothy, son of a Greek father and a Jewish mother. To avoid problems with Jewish converts, Paul has Timothy circumcised. They travel and preach with beautiful results. One night, at Troas, Paul has a vision: *"a man of Macedonia stood before him and invited him, 'Come over to Macedonia and help us.' After this vision, we immediately made efforts to get to Macedonia, concluding that God had summoned us to proclaim the good news there."*

Responsorial Psalm 100: 1-2, 3, 5

John 15: 18-21 *Jesus said to his disciples: "If you find that the world hates you, know it has hated me before you. The reason it hates you is that you do not belong to the world. But I chose you out of the world. Remember: no slave is greater than his master. They will harry you as they harried me. They will respect your words as much as they respected mine. All this they will do to you because of my name, for they know nothing of him who sent me."*

Reflection

The missionaries keep on truckin' through the Mediterranean, with wonderful results: *"Through all this, the congregations grew stronger in faith and daily increased in numbers."* Preaching trips planned for the province of Asia and into Bithynia do not pan out, but one night Paul receives a call to Macedonia in a vision. And when Luke reports *"we immediately made efforts to get across to Macedonia"* he's letting us know that he is now with Paul and has joined in the journey.

As part of his Farewell Discourse, Jesus warns the disciples they'll be facing the same difficulties that he underwent, and for the same reason. The world resents us because by following Christ we fly in the face of their ego-centered fantasies. Our values (and therefore our conduct) differ so greatly that they resent us being around, we remind them of other calls on their behavior and other choices they might/should be making. *"All this they will do to you because of my name."* Remember how the disciples gloried in being found so Christ-like that they were punished and suffered for the sake of his Name? How about us? Do we stand out enough from the world that we bother it, that we are ridiculed or even persecuted for our recognizably Christian behavior?

Sixth Sunday of Easter

Cycle A - Scripture

Acts of the Apostles 8: 5-8, 14-17 *Philip went to Samaria and there proclaimed the Messiah.* The crowds that heard him and saw his miracles listened closely to him. Many unclean spirits came out shrieking, and paralytics and cripples were also cured. *The rejoicing in that town rose to fever pitch.* When the church in Jerusalem heard that Samaria had accepted the word of God, they sent Peter and John over. They went, and prayed that the people might receive the Holy Spirit, because they had been baptized only in the name of the Lord Jesus. *The pair upon arriving imposed hands on them and they received the Holy Spirit.*

Responsorial Psalm 66: 1-3, 4-5, 6-7, 16, 20

First Letter of Peter 3: 15-18 *This is why Christ died for sins once for all, a just man for the sake of the unjust: so that he could lead you to God. He was put to death insofar as fleshly existence goes, but was given life in the realm of the spirit.*

John 14: 15-21 *Jesus said to his disciples: "If you love me and obey the commands I give you, I will ask the Father, and he will give you another Paraclete to be with you always—the Spirit of truth. He [will] remain with you and will be within you. He who obeys the commandments he has from me is the man who loves me; and he who loves me will be loved by my Father. I too will love him and reveal myself to him."*

Reflection

The Spirit marches on throughout this record of the early church's life. The deacon Philip gains converts in Samaria by his preaching and the

73

signs that accompany it. Since it is the baptism of Jesus, it is the sign of a willingness to follow, but it does not yet include the gift of the Spirit. So the church sends Peter and John to pray over them and lay hands on them. Sure enough, they all receive the Holy Spirit!

Peter, in his First Letter, expounds beautifully and clearly on the motive and the result of Jesus' saving death. He, the Just One, took on our sins so that he could rid us of them and lead us to God, now justified by him. But even as he gave over his life in this world for us, God returned it to him in the realm of the spirit, in the next world, by raising him anew to the glorious life he had left behind for our sakes.

Jesus will not leave us defenseless, he'll ask the Father to send us a new Paraclete (defense attorney, one who speaks on our behalf when we're in trouble), the Spirit, who not only will never leave us, but who will take up residence within us. Talk about being on call 24/7! Even Jesus' physical proximity to us cannot match this level of intimacy.

Sixth Sunday of Easter

Cycle B - Scripture

Acts of the Apostles 10: 25-26, 34-35, 44-48 *Peter entered the house of Cornelius and addressed them: "I begin to see how true it is that God shows no partiality. Rather, the man of any nation who fears God and acts uprightly is acceptable to him." Peter had not finished these words when the Holy Spirit descended upon all [his listeners]. The circumcised believers who had accompanied Peter were surprised that the gift of the Holy Spirit should have been poured out on the Gentiles also, whom they could hear speaking in tongues and glorifying God. Peter [asked], "What can stop these people who have received the Holy Spirit, even as we have, from* *being baptized with water?" So he gave orders that they be baptized in the name of Jesus Christ. After this was done, they asked him to stay with them for a few days.*

Responsorial Psalm 98: 1, 2-3, 3-4

First Letter of John 4: 7-10 *Beloved, let us love one another because love is of God; everyone who loves is begotten of God and has knowledge of God. The man without love has known nothing of God, for God is love. God's love was revealed in our midst in this way: he sent his only Son to the world that we might have life through him. Love, then, consists in this: not that we have loved God, but that he has loved us and has sent his Son as an offering for our sins.*

John 15: 9-17 (p. 69 & 70, Thursday & Friday of the Fifth Week of Easter)

Reflection

The Holy Spirit makes it easy for the disciples to decide. When he comes so visibly upon the Gentiles, in the same fashion as he had done with us, it's pretty clear we'd better step aside and let his grace have its way with them, as it has with us. Even so, it's traumatic for a Jew to shake off a lifetime of inherited and unquestioned prejudice against the Gentiles. It's another sign of the Spirit's power at work, that we are able to open our eyes and just drop the old ways that used to divide us.

There is nothing mushy about John's repeated use of the word "love." He takes it up to its highest power, and makes an awesome equation simple, something like Einstein moving from a whole blackboard full of mathematical symbols and logarithms to a stark and brief but world-shaking formulation: $E = mc2$. John says in several different ways that God is the source of love, the originator of our love relationship with him, that love is the source of our knowing anything truly important, and finally comes the simple but life-giving formulation: God = love. And since that equal sign works both ways, any love present in our lives makes God present in our lives.

Sixth Sunday of Easter

Cycle C - Scripture

Acts of the Apostles 15: 1-2, 22-29 (pp. 67 & 70, Wednesday & Friday 5th Week)

Responsorial Psalm 67: 2-3, 5, 6, 8

Revelation 21: 10-14, 22-23 *The angel carried me away* [writes St. John] *in spirit to the top of a high mountain and showed me the holy city Jerusalem coming down out of heaven from God. It gleamed with the radiance of a precious jewel like a diamond. The wall of the city had twelve courses of stones as its foundation, on which were written the names of the twelve apostles of the Lamb. I saw no temple in the city. The Lord God is its temple—he and the Lamb. The city had no need of sun or moon, for the glory of God gave it light, and its lamp was the Lamb.*

John 14: 23-29 (p. 65 & 66, Monday & Tuesday of the Fifth Week of Easter)

Reflection

John's vision of the Church Triumphant, the members of Christ's body already in heaven, is glorious, and full of precious details. It gleams like a diamond, for openers. It is built upon massive walls, with twelve gates at which twelve angels were stationed. The gates bore the names of the twelve tribes of Israel. The twelve courses of stone from which it rises bear the names of the twelve apostles of the Lamb. There is no temple building in the city, because the whole city is made sacred by the presence of the Lord God Almighty and the Lamb to the right of his throne. God's presence makes it shine, so it has no need of any lighting. The glory of God gave it light, and its lamp was the Lamb. The Holy Spirit is working overtime on the inspired description of this marvelous revelation. Makes you want to be there, doesn't it? And that's where Jesus went to prepare a place for us, so that where he was, we could be there with him! Hallelujah!

Monday of the Sixth Week of Easter

Scripture

Acts of the Apostles 16: 11-15 We arrived at Philippi, a Roman colony and leading city in the district of Macedonia. One Sabbath we went out to the river, looking for a place of prayer. We spoke to the women gathered there, and among our listeners was Lydia, a dealer in purple goods. Her heart was open to God, and she accepted Paul's message and was baptized, and said to them: *"If you are convinced that I believe in the Lord, come and stay at my house."* And they did.

Responsorial Psalm 149: 1-2, 3-4, 5-6, 9

John 15: 26 – 16: 4 *Jesus said to his disciples: "When the Paraclete comes, the Spirit of truth who comes from the Father, and whom I myself will send from the Father, he will bear witness on my behalf.*

You must bear witness as well. Not only will they expel you from synagogues; a time will come when anyone who puts you to death will claim to be serving God!"

Reflection

The purple dyes from this region were reputedly the best, so this Lydia is what we would call today a successful businesswoman. We know it because she can invite them, at the drop of a hat, to stay with her at her home. And the not-too-subtle way her invitation is phrased. Quite a gal. Quite a find, by the Holy Spirit, for this baby church to include a person of generosity and influence. Paul will later write a joyful letter to his beloved Philippians, the church he leaves behind after more time of preaching and conversion.

As he wraps up his words of farewell to his friends, Jesus warns them of the dangers looming ahead of them. In giving witness to what he has taught them, they will come upon the same rejection that was his lot, the same end that he came to. It's interesting that the only apostle to escape a martyr's death was John, of whom tradition says that the authorities, unsuccessful in trying to kill him by tossing him in a vat of boiling oil (with no results—he came out medium rare, at most), finally threw up their hands and simply said "Get him outta here!" and sent him off to exile on Patmos. He will die an old man, but not till after he has written a gospel, Revelation, and several letters to the churches. The Holy Spirit really knew what he was doing by sparing him.

Tuesday of the Sixth Week of Easter

Scripture

Acts of the Apostles 16: 22-34 When the crowd of Philippians turned on Paul and Silas, the magistrates seized them, flogged them, and threw them into prison, with instructions to have them guarded well. The jailer went so far as to have their feet chained to a stake. Long about midnight, while Paul and Silas are deep in prayer, a severe earthquake rocks the place. The doors fly open; everyone's chains are pulled loose. The jailer awakes to this sight and knows that if his prisoners are gone, his life is forfeit, so he reaches for his sword to do some hara-kiri. But Paul hastens to shout: *"Don't do it! We're all still here!" The jailer can hardly believe it. He falls at their feet, "Men, what must I do to be saved?" They answer, "Believe in the Lord Jesus and you will be saved, and all your household."* They announced the good news of Jesus to them right there, and the jailer responds by taking them into his house and bathing their wounds, receiving baptism, and joyfully spreading a table before them.

Responsorial Psalm 138: 1-2, 2-3, 7-8

John 16: 5-11 *Jesus said to his disciples: "Now that I go back to him who sent me, not one of you asks me, 'Where are you going?' Because I have [said] all this to you, you are overcome with grief. Yet I tell you the truth: It is much better for you that I go. If I fail to go, the Paraclete will never come to you, whereas if I go, I will send him to you. When he comes he will prove the world wrong."*

Reflection

It's a captivating story (get it?). The poor jailer figures the jig's up, but Paul is quick to assure him: "no prob!" What kind of men are these guys? When he asks them to explain themselves (and their wacko behavior), he receives a sermon right then and there. Their words find a home in him, and in turn he opens his home to them. Wounds are washed, wounded spirits are washed back to health in the blood of the Lamb, and after the baptism…some menudo—oops, forgot where I was—a party! What a wonderful ending to the story. And it's no wonder; the storyline is being written by the Spirit of Love.

Jesus sees their long faces coming on, but assures them it's for their own good that he's leaving, because not till he gets to heaven with his Father will they be sending down their Spirit, who bonds them in mutual love, to do the same for the disciples: bond them in filial love to that loving Father Jesus has revealed to them.

Wednesday of the Sixth Week of Easter

Scripture

Acts of the Apostles 17: 15, 22 – 18: 1 Paul went to Athens, and spoke out in the public square, telling them he was impressed by their religious zeal, since, beside all their other gods, they had an altar inscribed "To a God Unknown." He proceeded to make known to them this heretofore unknown God, who had created all things, and, as Lord of heaven and earth, didn't need a sanctuary made by human hands, nor words of adulation from men. Rather, it was he who gave life and breath to men and to all things living. If we are the result of his handiwork, we shouldn't think of divinity as a product of our hands, such as a statue. In the past God was satisfied that we bumbled along trying to know him. But now he has sent a man appointed, endorsed in the sight of all by being raised from the dead. At this, some sneered, while others expressed interest. A few joined him and became believers.

Responsorial Psalm 148: 1-2, 11-12, 13, 14

John 16: 12-15 *Jesus said to his disciples: "I have much more to tell you, but when he comes—the Spirit of truth—he will guide you to all truth. He will not speak on his own, but will speak only what he hears. He will have received from me what he will announce to you."*

Reflection

On his second missionary journey Paul brings the gospel of Jesus into Europe, by crossing over into Macedonia and Greece. Standing in the Areopagus in Athens, he is at the very center of learning and culture for the world of his day. His quick mind seizes the chance to comment on that altar "To a God Unknown" and off he goes, tracing true religion down the ages to the person of Jesus, raised from the dead by the Father. Now here's a God worth getting to know, so let me tell you about him. Go, Spirit, go!

Jesus is getting towards the end of his farewell, and realizes there's so much more he'd like to tell them. But he can do only so much. So he assures his disciples that the Spirit of truth that he will send them will bring them all truth, remind them of all that Jesus had taught them. Come, Spirit, come!

Thursday of the Sixth Week of Easter:

The Ascension of the Lord Jesus

(Please find readings on p. 86-89, from Sunday setting.)

Thursday of the Sixth Week of Easter

If the Ascension is celebrated not today, but next Sunday.

Scripture

Acts of the Apostles 18: 1-8 Paul left Athens and came to Corinth, where he met a fellow tent-maker, a Jew named Aquila, married to Priscilla. They took him in and he worked with them. Every Sabbath he'd speak up in the synagogue, in his zeal to convert both Jews and Greeks. When Silas and Timothy arrived from Macedonia, Paul gave himself full-time to the preaching of the word, testifying to the Jews that Jesus was the Christ. *When they opposed and reviled him, he shook out his garments and said, "Your blood be on your heads! I am clear of responsibility. From now on I will go to the Gentiles!"* So he went to the house of Titus Justus, a worshiper of God, who lived next door. And eventually Crispus, the synagogue official came to believe in the Lord, along with his entire household. Many of the Corinthians who heard also came to believe and were baptized.

Responsorial Psalm 98: 1, 2-3ab, 3cd-4

John 16: 16-20 *Jesus said to his disciples: "A little while and you will no longer see me, and again a little while later and you will see me." Some of his disciples said to one another, "What does this mean? What is this 'little while' of which he speaks?" Jesus knew they wanted to ask him, so he said to them, "Amen, I say to you, you will weep and mourn, while the world rejoices; you will grieve, but your grief will become joy."*

Reflection

Paul gives it his all, but to no avail. Rejected and reviled, he makes a formal end to the project, and moves away—next door! Sure enough, by hanging around the neighborhood he manages to convert the caretaker of the synagogue, with his entire household, as well as many other Corinthians.

Jesus is speaking in a veiled way of his death and momentary separation from his friends. The world, now, will think he's dead and gone—nuisance no more. His disciples will miss him dearly, they'll feel completely lost without him, but when he returns from death their hearts will jump for joy. Later, and this is the real context for these words—the prolonged physical separation from the Ascension to the Parousia—these words will console us and assure us of his presence through the Spirit.

Friday of the Sixth Week of Easter

Scripture

Acts of the Apostles 18: 9-18 One night in Corinth Paul had a vision of God telling him: *"Do not be afraid. Go on speaking and do* *not be silenced, for I am with you. No one will harm you."* But later the Jews rose in a body against him and brought him before the proconsul Gallio, accusing him of inducing people to break the law by the way he taught them to worship. Gallio quickly clarified his stance: if it were about a crime or a serious fraud, he would step in and judge. But since it was a dispute about their own religious law, he refused to be any part of it. So Paul continued in Corinth until it was time for him to sail for Syria, in the company of his old pals Aquila and Priscilla.

Responsorial Psalm 47: 2-3, 4-5, 6-7

John 16: 20-23 *Jesus said to his disciples: "You are sad for a time, but I shall see you again; then your hearts will rejoice with a joy no one can take from you. On that day you will have no questions to ask me."*

Reflection

Corinth is a tough place, a port where all types of people come ashore. Paul is assured of God's protection, but not of immunity from attack. Good ol' Gallio—I barely met him in this reading, but I like him already. He won't get suckered into this (religious) family squabble. Paul survived this crisis, and spent a total of eighteen months of preaching and teaching there. When he leaves, he does so with his oldest friends in town, Aquila and Priscilla, who you can bet are now involved in evangelizing along with him. Thank you, Holy Spirit.

Saturday of the Sixth Week of Easter

Scripture

Acts of the Apostles 18: 23-28 A Jew named Apollos arrived at Ephesus, an eloquent speaker, an authority on Scripture, and a teacher in the new way of the Lord. Though he knew only of John's baptism, he spoke and taught accurately and fearlessly about Jesus in their synagogues. Priscilla and Aquila heard him, and invited him home so they could explain to him God's new way in greater detail. He then went on to Achaia, where he was vigorous in refuting the Jewish party and in establishing from Scripture that Jesus was the Messiah.

Responsorial Psalm 47: 2-3, 8-9, 10

John 16: 23-28 *Jesus said to his disciples: "Whatever you ask the Father he will give you in my name. I have spoken these things to you in veiled language. A time will come when I shall no longer do so, but shall tell you about the Father in plain speech. The Father already loves you, because you have loved me and have believed that I came from God. I came into the world [from the Father]. Now I am leaving the world to go [back] to the Father."*

Reflection

The Book of Acts now begins the reporting on Paul's Third Missionary Journey, in Asia Minor. At the same time, the talented, charismatic Apollos begins to preach the good news of Jesus. It's interesting that Aquila and Priscilla, who had come into the picture as practicing Jews, hosts of Paul because they too were tentmakers, and later join him in his evangelizing work, now serve as the Spirit's instruments in preparing another powerful speaker to do his witnessing as well.

Jesus is still saying goodbye. He assures his friends that anything they ask the Father "in my name" will be granted by the Father, and not just because Jesus is our intercessor. He reveals plainly to us that the Father already loves us, because he sees the reception we have given his Son, sent to us out of love for us. Jesus, having convinced us of the Father's love for us, can now return home, having accomplished his mission. And the Spirit that the Father and the Son will send upon us will find a home in us, and remain in us, within us, as our most intimate friend, protector, advocate, and guide.

Seventh Sunday of Easter, when celebrating

The Ascension of the Lord

Scripture and Reflections

(A-B-C) Acts of the Apostles 1: 1-11 My first account dealt with all that Jesus did and taught until the day he was taken up to heaven, having first instructed the apostles through the Holy Spirit. In the time after his suffering he showed them in many convincing ways that he was alive, appearing to them over the course of forty days. On one occasion he told them not to leave Jerusalem: *"Wait, rather, for the fulfillment of my Father's promise. John baptized with water, but within a few days you will be baptized with the Holy Spirit. You will receive power when the Holy Spirit comes down on you, then you are to be my witnesses in Jerusalem, even to the ends of the earth."* No sooner had he said this than he was lifted up before their eyes in a cloud which took him from their sight.

Responsorial Psalm   47: 2-3, 6-7, 8-9

(A-B-C) Ephesians 1: 17-23 *May the God of our Lord Jesus Christ grant you a spirit of wisdom and insight to know him clearly…and the immeasurable scope of his power in us who believe. It is like the strength he showed in raising Christ from the dead and seating him at his right hand in heaven, high above every principality, power, virtue and domination, and every name that can be given in this age or the age to come. He has put all things under Christ's feet and has made him thus exalted, head of the church, which is his body, the fullness of him who fills the universe in all its parts.*

Cycle A - Scripture

Matthew 28: 16-20 The eleven made their way to Galilee [and] Jesus addressed them: *"Go and make disciples of all nations. Baptize them in the name 'of the Father, and of the Son, and of the Holy Spirit.' Teach them to carry out everything I have commanded you. And know that I am with you always, until the end of the world."*

Reflection

The end of the first Gospel commissions them to baptize and teach with the authority of Jesus himself, who will be with them, and with the church, till the end of time. The quotations around the Trinitarian formula in the text are explained in a footnote in the Jerusalem Bible: It may be that this formula, so far as the fullness of its expression is concerned, is a reflection of the liturgical usage established later in the primitive community, meaning that the words we've grown accustomed to using are placed on the lips of Jesus when this comes to be written down.

Cycle B - Scripture

Mark 16: 15-20 *[Jesus appeared to the Eleven and] said to them: "Go into the whole world and proclaim the good news to all* creation." Then the Lord Jesus was taken up into heaven and took his seat at God's right hand. The Eleven went forth and preached everywhere. The Lord continued to work with them throughout and confirm the message through the signs which accompanied them.

Reflection

This is the conclusion to the second Gospel. Notice how Mark interweaves the great events of Jesus' resurrection, ascension, exaltation, taking his place at the Father's right hand, and receiving the title "Lord." This title encompasses and caps off the whole career of Jesus; is now visibly present and at work through his disciples, in his church.

Cycle C - Scripture

Luke 24: 46-53 Jesus said to the Eleven: " *See, I send down upon you the promise of my Father. Remain here in the city until you are clothed with power from on high.*" He then led them out near Bethany, and blessed them. As he blessed, he left them, and was taken up to heaven.

Reflection

Luke's Jesus insists, both at the end of volume I (Gospel) and at the start of volume II (Acts), that the apostles wait in Jerusalem for the empowering by the Holy Spirit that the Father will send them. Jesus is closing the cover on his own book, but wants them ready for the next volume—the coming of the Spirit upon them. Looking back, it's pretty darned obvious, but that's hindsight for you. They will be quite surprised by the Spirit's arrival, in the loud wind blowing and the tongues as of fire settling over them. The <u>real</u> surprise, of course, will be for the world. "Who are those guys?" (a la Sundance Kid) –

there's no stopping them! Our timorous, cowering disciples are coming bravely into the open and preaching their heads off, once the Spirit's power has been unleashed in them.

Paul sings a hymn of lyric praise to Jesus, the head of the body of believers, raised from the dead, and now raised from earth to heaven, so he can be seen in his rightful place—at the right hand of God, over every creature, filling the entire universe with the glory that the Father has given him.

A historical aside:
The entire 50-day period following Easter was originally called Pentecost (in Greek, fiftieth {day is understood}, in Latin Quinquagesima) but over time the first 40 days were considered a sort of after-Lent, the time of the risen Christ with his disciples until his Ascension. The last 10 days form a prelude for the descent of the Holy Spirit. Prior to this partitioning, Easter was considered to contain the entire paschal mystery: death, resurrection, ascension, and the sending of the Spirit.

Seventh Sunday of Easter

When the Ascension was celebrated last Thursday

Cycle A - Scriptures

Acts of the Apostles 1: 12-14 *[After Jesus was taken up into the heavens,] the apostles returned to Jerusalem [and] went to the upstairs room where they were staying: Peter and John and James and Andrew; Philip and Thomas, Bartholomew and Matthew; James son of Alpheus, Simon the Zealot party member, and Judas son of James. Together they devoted themselves to constant prayer. There* *were some women in their company and Mary the mother of Jesus, and his brothers.*

Responsorial Psalm 27: 1, 4, 7-8

First Letter of Peter 4: 13-16 *Rejoice, insofar as you share Christ's sufferings. When his glory is revealed you will rejoice exultantly. Happy are you when you are insulted for the sake of Christ, for then God's Spirit in its glory has come to rest on you. See to it that none of you suffers for [doing evil]. If anyone suffers for being a Christian, however, he ought not be ashamed. He should rather glorify God in virtue of that name.*

John 17: 1-11 *Jesus looked up to heaven and said: "Father, the hour has come! Glorify your Son, that your Son may glorify you. I have glorified you on earth by doing what you gave me to do. Now you, Father, give me glory at your side once more, the glory I had with you before the world began. I have made your name known to those you gave me out of the world. I entrusted to them the message you entrusted to me, and they received it. They accept that in truth I came from you, they believe it was you who sent me. For them I pray—not for the world but for those you gave me. I am in the world no longer, but they are in the world as I come to you."*

Reflection

After watching Jesus vanish into the heavens, the apostolic band gathers once again in the upper room, along with Mary and some other women disciples, and devote themselves to intense prayer. How they must have wondered what would happen next! What would they do without their leader? Surely that awful hole left in them by his death had been more than filled with the joy of his return from the dead, and the many occasions on which he had shown himself to them. But now…what? No wonder they turned to prayer. There was nothing in their power to do—it was all up to God.

Peter writes to strengthen the persecuted, suffering disciples. Be glad you suffer with Christ, on his account, because that means that God's Spirit in its glory has come to rest on you, the same as Jesus. What a blessing, to know yourself the enemy of the world precisely because you so clearly demonstrate the presence of Jesus in you, the same Jesus the world hated and rejected before it hated and rejected you.

Jesus has given God glory by his life of total dedication to the Father's will. He has taken us up out of sin and linked us to the holiness of the Father, the glory to which he will soon return, having carried out his task. We will remain behind in his place, with his Spirit helping us in that same task: to witness to his life, to offer and bring about the salvation of those other sheep he leaves that are not yet in his flock. He prays for us to do as he has done. Amen. Amen. May it be so!

Seventh Sunday of Easter

Cycle B - Scriptures

Acts of the Apostles 1: 15-17, 20-26 Peter stood and addressed the one hundred and twenty or so disciples gathered together. He quoted Psalm 109, verse 8: "May another take his place," to justify the step he proposed next. "Since Judas had gone his way, we should nominate someone who has accompanied us all the way from the baptism of John to the day Jesus was taken from us, to take his place among the Twelve." Lots were cast between Joseph (called Barsabbas, also known as Justus) and Matthias. Thankfully, we were spared the profusion of names, and the lot fell to Matthias, who was immediately added to (round out) the Twelve.

Responsorial Psalm 103: 1-2, 11-12, 19-20

First Letter of John 4: 11-16 *Beloved, if God has loved us so, we must have the same love for one another. No one has ever seen God. Yet if we love one another God dwells in us, and his love is brought to perfection in us. The way we know we remain in him and he in us is that he has given us of his Spirit. God is love, and he who abides in love abides in God, and God in him.*

John 17: 11-19 *Jesus looked up to heaven and prayed: "Most holy Father, protect them, that they may be one, even as we are one. I gave them your word, and the world has hated them for it; they do not belong to the world any more than I do. I do not ask you to take them out of the world, but to guard them from the evil one. As you have sent me into the world, so I have sent them into the world. I consecrate myself for their sakes now, that they may be consecrated in truth."*

Reflection

One of the first things the church did was to make up for the loss of Judas from their group. Note how they use simple methods (drawing straws, casting lots) because they trust God will reveal his will in the resulting choice. It was important to restore the proper number (highly symbolic and historically meaningful) to show that God's plans can never be thwarted. They trusted in God, but they did their homework, too: the candidates had to have shared in Jesus' work and company all the way from the first move, the baptism in the Jordan, to the last one, death on the cross, to ensure a legitimate continuity.

There is an elegant simplicity in these phrases from John's first letter, that can perhaps be explained by the fact that when John comes to write them, he is an old man; his thought has been distilled, so that distractions are left aside and the spotlight falls on just the important message. There's a story that when he became not just older but quite feeble, John was still so loved by his people that at their Eucharistic celebrations they would bring him out in a chair to address them, and that he would simply say: "Little children, love one another." That's it. Over and out. So there you have it, in capsule form: "God is love. When you live in love, you're living in God…and God is living in you." What more do we have to know in order to live good Christian lives?

In his High-Priestly Prayer Jesus consecrates his followers to the Father's service, to bringing God's truth, his loving message, to the world, even if the world hates them for it. No surprise, the world has hated Christ because it finds his message so subversive of its warped values. So will it hate anyone else who preaches and lives out that same message that calls for making room for God by making room for others in our lives. How can I take care of myself if I waste my time caring for others? Doesn't make sense….

Seventh Sunday of Easter

Cycle C - Scriptures

Acts of the Apostles 7: 55-60 (p. 36, Tuesday of the Third Week of Easter)

Responsorial Psalm 97: 1-2, 6-7, 9

Revelation 22: 12-14, 16-17, 20 *I, John, heard a voice saying to me: "Remember, I am coming soon! I bring with me the reward that will be given to each man as his conduct deserves. It is I, Jesus, who have sent my angel to give you this testimony about the churches. The Spirit and the Bride say, "Come!" Let him who hears answer, "Come!" Let him who is thirsty come forward; let all who desire it accept the gift of life-giving water. The One who gives this testimony says, "Yes, I am coming soon!" Amen! Come, Lord Jesus!*

John 17: 20-26 *Jesus looked up to heaven and said: "I do not pray for my disciples alone. I pray also for those who will believe in me through their word, that all may be one as you, Father, are in me, and I in you. I have given them the glory you gave me, that they may be one, as we are one—I living in them, you living in me—that their unity may be complete. So shall the world know that you sent me, and that you loved them as you loved me. These men have known that you sent me. To them I have revealed your name, and I will continue to reveal it, so that your love for me may live in them, and I may live in them."*

Reflection

John's vision has Jesus assuring his persecuted brothers and sisters that victory will be theirs, that he's coming with water for the thirsty, food for the hungry, strength for the weak, victory for the vanquished…and soon! This selection from <u>Revelation</u> is the end of the last book of the Bible, so: "Come, Lord Jesus!" are the words on which the Bible ends. Nice dynamic closing punch!

This Gospel passage also is the end: the end of Jesus' High-Priestly Prayer for his close friends. The very next verse begins chapter 18, with the arrest of Jesus leading up to his passion and death. So Jesus lets it all hang out, as they say, he holds nothing back. He asks for unity between them and himself, to match the unity between himself and the Father. Of course, the Bond of Union between Father and Son is nothing less than the Holy Spirit! His last request in this prayer is: "that your love may live in them, and I may live in them." Amen!

Monday of the Seventh Week of Easter

Scripture

Acts of the Apostles 19: 1-8 Paul came to Ephesus and asked some disciples if they had received the Holy Spirit when they became believers. They answered, *"We have not so much as heard that there is a Holy Spirit."* *"Well, how were you baptized?"* he persisted. *"With the baptism of John,"* they replied. So Paul explained to them how John was preparing for the one who would come after him, that is, Jesus. They immediately asked for baptism in the name of Jesus, and when Paul laid his hands on them, they received the Holy Spirit and began speaking in tongues and prophesying.

Responsorial Psalm 68: 2-3, 4-5, 6-7

John 16: 29-33 *The disciples said to Jesus: "At last you are speaking plainly without talking in veiled language! We do believe you came from God." Jesus answered them: "Do you really believe? An hour is coming—has indeed already come—when you will be scattered and each will go his way, leaving me quite alone. (Yet I can never be alone; the Father is with me.) I tell you all this that in me you may find peace. You will suffer in the world. But take courage! I have overcome the world."*

Reflection

The Holy Spirit continues to be the protagonist in Luke's story of the early church's life. Paul is led by the Spirit to some ("about twelve men in all") who are still on the verge. They are disciples, they are following the way of Jesus, but not until Paul lays hands on them do they receive, and give proof of, the presence and power and gifts of the Holy Spirit: speaking in tongues and prophesying, that is, speaking out on God's behalf, announcing his message to the church.

So you think you've got it all figured out? Jesus lets them know he is aware of future denials in crucial situations. But he assures them he can take it: others' word may waver, but his Father's is rock-solid. He can count on his Father—always. In upcoming temptations, you will suffer, he tells them, and may therefore falter. But there'll be no faltering from me, because thanks to the Father's constancy (and to the Spirit who conveys it to me) I have overcome the world.

Tuesday of the Seventh Week of Easter

Scripture

Acts of the Apostles 20: 17-27 Paul called together the elders of the church at Ephesus and told them: *"You know how I lived among you from the first day I set foot in the province of Asia—how I served the Lord in humility through the sorrows and trials that came my way from the plottings of certain Jews. Never did I shrink from telling you what was for your own good. With Jews and Greeks alike I insisted in repentance before God and on faith in our Lord Jesus."* "But now you see me," he continued, "on my way to Jerusalem, at the Spirit's urging, even though I'm being warned that chains and hardships await me. I know that we won't see each other again, so I'm using this occasion to declare openly that I accept no blame for anyone's conscience, because I have always announced God's design to you in its entirety, for good or ill."

John 17: 1-11 (p. 90, Seventh Sunday of Easter, Cycle "A")

Reflection

Paul is clearing up accounts, getting everything off his chest, as he prepares to depart and not return. He reminds them of his humble, painful start among them, and how he never lacked the courage to confront them over irregularities in their behavior or misunderstandings of his teaching. He has always tried to be faithful to the Holy Spirit's call, even now as it hints of danger ahead. All he hopes to accomplish is to *"complete the service to which I have been assigned by the Lord Jesus, bearing witness to the gospel of God's grace."* As he leaves with no prospect of returning, he can in good conscience state that he has done his job, he has always announced God's design to them in its entirety.

Wednesday of the Seventh Week of Easter

Scripture

Acts of the Apostles 20: 28-38 Paul addressed the elders of the church at Ephesus: *"Keep watch over yourselves, and over the whole flock the Holy Spirit has given you to guard. Shepherd the church of God, which he has acquired at the price of his own blood. I know that when I am gone, savage wolves will come among you who will not spare the flock."* Some of your own members will distort the truth and try to lead the people astray. Don't forget how I've always tried to warn you. *I commend you to the Lord, and to that gracious* *word of his which can enlarge you, and give you a share among all who are consecrated to him.* You know how I never wasted my time on coveting anyone's money or fine clothing. Instead I've always worked with my own hands to meet my needs and those of my companions. I've always pointed out to you that it's by your hard work that you must help the weak in your midst. Remember the words of Jesus: *'There is more happiness in giving than receiving.'*"

After this discourse, Paul knelt down with them all and prayed. They began to weep without restraint, throwing their arms around him and kissing him, for they were deeply distressed to hear that they would never see his face again.

Responsorial Psalm 68: 29-30, 33-35, 35-36

John 17: 11-19 (p. 92, Seventh Sunday of Easter, Cycle "B")

Reflection

Paul really lays on the advice to his friends, knowing that this is virtually his last chance to address them face-on. He charges the shepherds in positions of leadership to remain careful to their precious charge of guarding the flock in the name of the Shepherd. He reminds them of the example he had worked hard to leave them, hard-working and constant. Then, in a touching scene, they tearfully take leave of each other.

Thursday of the Seventh Week of Easter

Scripture

Acts of the Apostles 22: 30; 23: 6-11 The commander summoned the chief priests and the whole Sanhedrin to a meeting, and brought in Paul to stand before them and defend himself against his charges. Paul knew that, of the group, some were Pharisees and others Sadducees, so he opened with this statement: *"Brothers, I am a Pharisee and was born a Pharisee. I find myself on trial now because of my hope in the resurrection of the dead."* Right then and there a heavy dispute broke out, since the Sadducees maintain there is no resurrection, while the Pharisees say there is. A loud uproar resulted from this opening salvo. Finally, some of the Pharisees declared: *"We do not find this man guilty of any crime."* At this, the dispute grew worse, and the commander, fearing that they would tear Paul to pieces, removed him for his own safety. *That night the Lord appeared at Paul's side and said: "Keep up your courage! Just as you have given testimony to me here in Jerusalem, so must you do in Rome."*

Responsorial Psalm 16: 1-2, 5, 7-8, 9-10, 11

John 17: 20-26 (p. 94, Seventh Sunday of Easter, Cycle "C")

Reflection

Paul has ended his Third Missionary Journey at the temple in Jerusalem. Arrested there, he defends himself before the Sanhedrin, the 70-member Jewish Senate. Paul uses the resurrection-card to stir up the members against each other, resulting in such chaos that the commander feels forced to remove Paul physically from their midst. Jesus will come to Paul in a vision that night, and announce his plans for Paul's witnessing to him in Rome, the capital of the whole world!

Friday of the Seventh Week of Easter

Scripture

Acts of the Apostles 25: 13-21 King Agrippa and his sister Bernice arrived in Caesarea and paid Festus, the Roman Procurator, a courtesy call. And, since they'd be there a few days, Festus referred Paul's case to the king's judgment. "In my absence the chief priests and elders of the Jews brought charges against this man, demanding his condemnation. Later I told them it was not the Roman way to hand over an accused man without allowing him to face his accusers to defend himself. But they charged him with nothing I had expected; instead, their differences were over religious issues, about a certain Jesus who had been put to death but who Paul claimed was alive. I offered to send the case back to Jerusalem, but Paul appealed for an imperial investigation."

Responsorial Psalm 103: 1-2, 11-12, 19-20

John 21: 15-19 (p. 33, Third Sunday of Easter, Cycle "C")

Reflection

The Agrippa-Bernice duo serves to elicit the story from Festus. He finds it interesting, and figures his royal guests will also. Paul, as any Roman citizen would, claims his right to be judged by Rome, rather than by any rustic venue with hayseed defenders. Actually, Paul is aware the religious authorities in Jerusalem would love to dispose of him, so Rome is not only a no-brainer, it's also a life-saver. And, in God's providence, Rome will provide the "bully pulpit" for Paul to reach out to the whole world; after all, "All roads lead to—and from—Rome." He will spend the rest of his days in minimum security conditions, free to receive visitors and writing paper, lots of writing paper.

Saturday of the Seventh Week of Easter

Scripture

Acts of the Apostles 28: 16-20, 30-31 *Upon entry into Rome, Paul was allowed to take a lodging of his own, although a soldier was assigned to keep guard over him. For two full years Paul stayed on in his rented lodgings, welcoming all who came to him. With full assurance, and without any hindrance whatever, he preached the reign of God and taught about the Lord Jesus Christ.*

Responsorial Psalm 11: 4, 5, 7

John 21: 20-25 *As Peter followed Jesus, he noticed that the disciple whom Jesus loved was [also] following. [This] prompted [him] to ask Jesus, "Lord, what about him?" "Suppose I want him to stay until I come," Jesus replied, "how does that concern you?" This is how the report spread among the brothers that this disciple was not going to die. It is this same disciple who is the witness to these things; it is he who wrote them down and his testimony, we know, is true. There are still many other things that Jesus did, yet if they were written about in detail, I doubt there would be room enough in the entire world to hold the books to record them."*

Reflection

Actually, it turns out Paul was not even in mini-minimum security: he got to live in his own place (some rented digs—Romans were pretty slick: that way the prisoner had to cover his own expenses, even as he was provided with a live-in "ankle bracelet" guard). The point is that, after all these attempts to silence him, Paul is sitting pretty in Rome, the hub of the entire empire, teaching and preaching away in complete freedom, and getting off letters to the churches he had set in place on his journeys. (And I'm betting that guard didn't take too long to come around, either.)

Today's gospel selection is the conclusion of John's gospel. (Interesting that there must have been rumors that John—he was getting pretty darn old: in his 90's in those days of not-so-many-years of life expectancy—was not going to die, just hang around until Jesus came back in power and majesty.) John, in his typically modest way, claims eyewitness authenticity for his gospel, and explains that he simply had to leave out a lot of what Jesus said and did. But the implication is that what he did include is so that we readers can share the experiences that he and the other apostles shared with Jesus, and the impact Jesus and his Spirit made on them.

The Vigil of Pentecost

Scripture

(A-B-C) Four choices for the first reading:

1st – Genesis 11: 1-9 *At that time the whole world spoke the same language. [The people] said, "Let us build ourselves a city and a tower with its top in the sky, and so make a name for ourselves;*

otherwise we shall be scattered all over the earth." The Lord came down to see [it and] said, "If now, while they are one people, speaking the same language, they have started to do this, nothing will later stop them from doing whatever they presume to do. Let us then go down and confuse their language, so that no one will understand what another says." That is why it was called Babel, because there the Lord confused the speech of all the world [and] scattered them all over the earth.

2nd – Exodus 19: 3-8, 16-20 *Moses went up the mountain to God. The Lord said, "Tell the Israelites: 'You have seen for yourselves how I treated the Egyptians and how I bore you up on eagle wings and brought you here to myself. If you hearken to my voice and keep my covenant, you shall be my special possession, dearer to me than all other people.'" So Moses went and summoned the people. When he [told] them all that the Lord had ordered, the people all answered together, "Everything the Lord has said, we will do." On the third day Moses led the people out of the camp to meet God, and they stationed themselves at the foot of Mount Sinai [which] was all wrapped in smoke, for the Lord came down upon it in fire, and the whole mountain trembled violently.*

3rd – Ezekiel 37: 1-14 *The hand of the Lord led me out in the spirit of the Lord and set me in the center of the plain, which was filled with bones. He said to me: Prophesy over these bones, and say to them: Dry bones, hear the word of the Lord! Thus says the Lord God to these bones: I will bring spirit into you, that you may come to life. I will put sinews upon you, make flesh grow over you, cover you with skin, and put spirit in you so that you may come to life and know that I am the Lord. As I was prophesying I heard a noise; it was a rattling as the bones came together. I saw the sinews and the flesh come upon them, and the skin cover them, but there was no spirit in them. Then he said to me: Prophesy and say to the spirit: Thus says the Lord God: Come, O spirit, and breathe into these slain that they may come to life. And the spirit came into them; they came alive and stood upright, a vast army. Then he said to me: These bones are the whole* house of Israel. They have been saying, "Our bones are dried up, our hope is lost, and we are cut off." Say to them: Thus says the Lord: O my people, I will open your graves and have you rise from them, and bring you back to the land of Israel. Then you shall know that I am the Lord. I will put my spirit in you that you may live, and I will settle you upon your land, thus you shall know that I am the Lord. I have promised, and I will do it, says the Lord.

4th – Joel 3: 1-5 *Thus says the Lord: I will pour out my spirit upon all mankind. / Your sons and daughters shall prophesy, your old men shall dream dreams, your young men shall see visions; / even upon the servants and handmaids I will pour out my spirit. / The sun will be turned to darkness, and the moon to blood, / at the coming of the Day of the Lord, the great and terrible day. / Then everyone shall be rescued who calls on the name of the Lord; / for on Mount Zion there shall be a remnant, as the Lord has said, / and in Jerusalem survivors whom the Lord shall call.*

Responsorial Psalm 104: 1-2, 24, 27-28, 29, 30

Romans 8:22-27 *The Spirit helps us in our weakness, for we do not know how to pray as we ought; but the Spirit himself makes intercession for us with groanings which cannot be expressed in speech. He who searches hearts knows what the Spirit means, for the Spirit intercedes for the saints as God himself wills.*

John 7:37-39 *Jesus [said], "If anyone thirsts, let him come to me; let him drink. Scripture has it: 'From within him rivers of living water shall flow.'" (He was referring to the Spirit, whom those that came to believe in him were to receive.   There was no Spirit as yet, since Jesus had not yet been glorified.)*

Reflection

1st – At Pentecost, the Holy Spirit will become the unifier of all people, by undoing the Babel experience. The language of God's love will overcome all barriers and gather all people from the world over into the one flock under one Shepherd.

2nd – At Pentecost, without the smoke and trembling, the Holy Spirit will establish a new covenant with the new people of God, Jesus' little band of followers all gathered in the upper room. The tongues of fire clearly supply the sign of God's approving partnership.

3rd – At Pentecost, God's breath of life, his spirit, will blow over the lifeless panorama of this sinful world, and bring a new life—God's own—into what without him would be just a bunch of old bleached bones lying around. We <u>can</u> come back from our sins: "I have promised, and I will do it, says the Lord."

4th – The Lord promises: "I will pour out my spirit upon all mankind. Your sons and daughters shall prophesy, your old men shall dream dreams, your young men shall see visions." And in case you thought he was being stingy with his spirit, "Even upon the servants and the handmaids, I will pour out my spirit." Does that about cover it? God wants to share his life-giving breath (the Spirit) with <u>everyone</u>.

St. Paul reassures us, that even if we can't do as good a job of praying as we should, the Holy Spirit within us takes over and goes above and beyond what the finest of human words could accomplish. He's on the same frequency as the Father, who reads him like a lovely book.

At the festival of Tabernacles (Booths) there is a blessing of God for his gift of water, the most precious commodity for desert dwellers. From this background comes Jesus' allusion to rivers of living water, likely hearkening back to Ezekiel's vision of the water that begins as a trickle from the Temple door and then becomes a mighty, life-giving river (chapter 47). We also remember Jesus in conversation with the

Samaritan woman at the well in John's chapter 4, assuring her of never-ending supplies of living water.

At Calvary John (19: 35) will make much of the water he witnessed coming out of Jesus' pierced heart.   St. Paul will establish a powerful image, connecting the life-giving waters of baptism with the "pouring out" of the Holy Spirit upon us.

The Feast of Pentecost

Scripture

(A-B-C)

Acts of the Apostles 2: 1-11 *[On] the day of Pentecost the brethren [were] gathered in one place. Suddenly from up in the sky there came a noise like a strong, driving wind which was heard throughout the house. Tongues as of fire appeared which parted and came to rest on each of them. All were filled with the Holy Spirit. They began to express themselves in foreign tongues and make bold proclamations as the Spirit prompted them. Staying in Jerusalem at the time were devout Jews of every nation under heaven. These heard the sound, and assembled in a large crowd. They were much confused because each of them heard these men speaking his own language. The whole occurrence astonished them.*

Responsorial Psalm 104: 1, 24, 29-30, 31, 34

1 Corinthians 12: 3-7, 12-13 *No one can say, "Jesus is Lord," except by the Holy Spirit. There are different kinds of spiritual gifts but the same Spirit; there are different workings but the same God who produces all of them in everyone. For in one Spirit we were all* *baptized into one body, whether Jews or Greeks, slaves or free persons, and we were all given to drink of one Spirit.*

(alternate second reading) Romans 8: 8-17 *If Christ is in you, although the body is dead because of sin, the spirit is alive because of righteousness. If the Spirit of the one who raised Jesus from the dead dwells in you, the one who raised Christ from the dead will give life to your mortal bodies also, through his Spirit that dwells in you. Those who are led by the Spirit of God are sons of God. For you did not receive a spirit of slavery to fall back into fear, but you received a spirit of adoption, through whom we cry, "Abba, Father!"*

John 20: 19-23 *On the evening of that first day of the week, Jesus came and said to them, "Peace be with you. As the Father has sent me, so I send you." [Then] he breathed on them and said, "Receive the Holy Spirit."*

(alternate Gospel reading) John 14: 15-16, 23-26 *Jesus said to his disciples: "I will ask the Father, and he will give you another Advocate to be with you always. Whoever loves me will keep my word, and my Father will love him, and we will come to him and make our dwelling with him. I have told you this while I am with you. The Advocate, the Holy Spirit whom the Father will send in my name, will teach you everything and remind you of all that I told you."*

Background

The term "economy of salvation" was coined centuries ago by theologians to describe the activity of God in the working out of our salvation. They speak of the three eras, or stages, in accord with the activity of each of the three Persons of God. The first is the age of the Father, whose main role is creation. Then, at the appointed time, Jesus appears in our history as our redeemer. Whereas the era of the Creator covered eons, the era of the Redeemer comprised just around thirty-some years. Not a lot of time, but a very concentrated dose of salvation! Finally, we come to the age of the Spirit, whose role is to be our Sanctifier. Only God knows how long this period will go on, but we know when it started: when Jesus left us to go to the Father and send us another Paraclete (Advocate), who would take over the work in its plan C. Interesting, no?

Obviously, all three Persons in the Trinity share intimately in all of God's work, but, for purposes of discussion and analysis, we have to use our limited (and therefore limiting) human thought patterns. Thus we "separate" the activities of the three divine Persons into neat packets that allow us to "capture" a little bit of clarification. We could, of course, just throw up our hands and say it's all a mystery, but I think it's good for us to use the brains God gave us and try to advance in our understanding of the Trinitarian mystery—the most basic truth about God revealed to us. We now return to our regularly scheduled program.

Reflection

In his gospel and the Book of Acts, St. Luke has produced a two-volume set on the activity of the Holy Spirit. The first deals with the Spirit at work in Jesus: present at his conception, at his presentation at the temple, at the baptism which opens his career, all through his life, and returned to the Father's hands at the moment of Jesus' death. The second volume charters the same activities of the same Spirit in the not-quite-the-same Jesus: the Jesus who lives in his body, the church. Today's Acts 2 marks the birthday of the church as we exist today: Jesus seemingly absent but powerfully and sacramentally present in the actions of his body, the assembly of his followers who constitute his real, bodily, corporate presence by the action of his Spirit at work in us.

In Acts 2 we see the antidote for Genesis 11's scattering of humanity into different language groups ("he has scattered the proud in their conceit"). Now begins the great project of the re-unifying of the whole world ("to the ends of the earth" we are to witness), based on the Spirit's power at work in us. Isn't the job of the Holy Spirit to be the glue of love between Father and Son? Doesn't the Spirit provide the same wonderful effect for us when we become brothers and sisters of Jesus?

St. Paul's first selection reminds us that the same God is the source of our life, and of all our gifts. We are given these gifts, not for an exclusive use/enjoyment, but for the good of all the members of the one body we form by being "all baptized into one body." Caught up in the language of baptismal imagery, he liquefies the ethereal breath of God into the living water "we were all given to drink."

In Romans 8 we are swept up into the Trinitarian life of God. Since Christ is in us, the Spirit in which he was raised up from death by the Father will also raise us up. Thus, the Spirit we've received is a spirit of adoption, making us sons and daughters of God just as truly as Jesus is God's Son! This opens our approach of filial love for God, so we "dare to say" (as the intro to the Lord's Prayer encourages): not "Your Excellency," or "Sovereign Lord," or "Omnipotent, All-knowing Majesty, Who maintainest all things in their proper order…" but simply and lovingly "Abba, Father!" Ah, the Spirit, bond of love!

John 19 makes the meaning of the word "spirit" transparent: Jesus breathes on us and says, "Receive the Holy Spirit (the Holy Breath of Life…and not just human life, but the life that the Father and I share)." Mi casa es su casa.

In John 14, Jesus is preparing his disciples (unsuccessfully, as usual) for his "leaving" them behind. Poor babies, they were crushed when his death took him from them, elated when he returned, and loath to see him go away again. But how consoling is the promise of Jesus "my Father will love him, and we will come to him and make our dwelling with him" (emphasis added). Remember that lovely phrase of yesteryear—the Indwelling of the Holy Spirit? That's what the Spirit does for us as our Sanctifier: he introduces us into the Trinitarian life of God, here and now, right in the middle of this messy world!

This is why we can say (and mean): Jesus Christ is Lord! The Creator is my <u>Abba!</u> Thank you, Holy Spirit.

And now it is my bittersweet duty to remind us (I feel like the guy who put the last stone on the Taj Mahal—hey, great! but now it's all over….) that we've come to the end of the great Paschal season, the Church's great retreat, that got us on board all the way from Ash Wednesday along the sorrowful but purposeful journey with Jesus, through the intense events of Palm Sunday and the Triduum, and—onward and upward!—along the way of Jesus raised from death and rising to heaven, to send us the Spirit, the mission of his entire life's work. Pentecost is not an isolated feast. It was the motive for Jesus' work as Redeemer, so he could pass on the baton as we pass over into our new Christian life in the Spirit, the Sanctifier. The Pentecostal arrival of the Holy Spirit, who picks up where Christ left off, marks the beginning of the final stage of our life, the birth of the church. Happy Birthday, everybody! Alleluia! Amen.

P.S. Feasts that are to be celebrated <u>on fixed dates</u> in the Mystagogia season:

April 25th: St. Mark, Evangelist

Scriptures

First Letter of Peter 5: 5-14 *Bow humbly under God's mighty hand, so that in due time he may lift you high. Resist [the devil], solid in your faith, realizing that the brotherhood of believers is undergoing the same sufferings throughout the world. The God of all grace, who called you to his everlasting glory in Christ, will himself restore,* *confirm, strengthen and establish those who have suffered a little while. Dominion be his through the ages! Amen. The church in Babylon sends you greeting, as does Mark my son. Greet one another with the embrace of true love. To all of you who are in Christ, peace.*

Responsorial Psalm 89: 2-3, 6-7, 16-17

Mark 16: 15-20 *Jesus appeared to the Eleven and said, "Go into the world and proclaim the good news to all creation. Signs like these will back up those who profess their faith: they will expel demons in my name, they will handle serpents safely, drink deadly poison without harm, and the sick upon whom they lay hands will recover."* Then the Lord Jesus was taken up into heaven to sit at God's right hand. The Eleven went forth and preached everywhere, with the Lord confirming their message through the signs that accompanied them.

Reflection

The first reading comes into play because, in parting, it includes regards from the church at Rome (Babylon was a code name for the capital of the evil empire that was persecuting them) and from Mark, Peter's companion in Rome. From this vantage point, Mark played a role in the developing young church. His main contribution, obviously, is his work, pioneering the whole genre of gospel (the good news about Jesus). Born in Jerusalem, he accompanied Barnabas, Paul and Peter in their evangelizing. Peter was such an influence on young John Mark (as he was first known) that his gospel is sometimes referred to as the gospel of Peter. It certainly bears his stamp: brusque, close to the people on the street, mincing no words, direct. The gospel selection comes from the "longer ending" among the several traditional endings for his gospel.

May 3rd: Saints Philip and James, Apostles

Scripture

First Corinthians 15: 1-8 *Brothers, I want to remind you of the gospel I preached to you, which you received and in which you stand firm. You are being saved by it at this very moment if you retain it as I preached it to you. I handed on to you first of all what I myself received, that Christ died for our sins in accord with the Scriptures; that he was buried and, in accord with the Scriptures, rose on the third day; that he was seen by Cephas, then by the Twelve. After that he was seen by five hundred brothers at once, most of whom are still alive. Next he was seen by James; then by all the apostles. Last of all he was seen by me, as one born out of the normal course.*

Responsorial Psalm 19: 2-3, 4-5

John 14: 6-14 (p. 58, Saturday of the Fourth Week of Easter)

Reflection

Saints Philip and James are honored together because in Rome the Church of the Twelve Apostles has relics of these two under its main altar, and it was on this date, in 565, that this church was dedicated. Philip came from Bethsaida, on the shores of Lake Genesaret (Galilee). James the Less, son of Alpheus is considered in tradition to be the cousin of Jesus who later played a role of leadership in the Jerusalem church, when Peter set off on mission and ended up in Rome. He is also considered to be the author of the blunt, strong <u>Letter of James</u> in the New Testament. Because special mention is made of him in this selection from Paul, it figures naturally in the readings of his feastday.

May 14th: St. Mathias, Apostle

Scripture

Acts of the Apostles 1: 15-17, 20-26 (p. 91, Seventh Sunday of Easter, Cycle "B")

Responsorial Psalm 113: 1-2, 3-4, 5-6, 7-8

John 15: 9-17 (p. 69 & 70, Thursday & Friday of the Fifth Week of Easter)

Reflection

Concerning St. Mathias we know only that, during the time between the Ascension and Pentecost, he was elected as an Apostle, to maintain the powerful symbolism of the Twelve hand-picked by Jesus, echoing the twelve tribes of the Father's hand-picked people, figured so richly in visions such as in the Book of Revelation, etc. Mathias took the place vacated by Judas, making up for his betrayal and desertion. Since he was selected by the casting of lots, guess which Apostle is the patron saint of Las Vegas, Nevada? Feeling lucky? Take a chance….